D0344410

Chicken

Chicken

DISCARD

Self-Portrait of
a Young Man for Rent

David Henry Sterry

ReganBooks
An Imprint of **HarperCollins**Publishers

306.743
S839c

Some names and characters have been changed to protect them and me.

CHICKEN. Copyright © 2002 by David Henry Sterry.

All rights reserved. Printed in the United States of America.
No part of this book may be used or reproduced in any manner whatsoever
without written permission except in the case
of brief quotations embodied in critical articles and reviews.
For information address HarperCollins Publishers Inc.,
10 East 53rd Street, New York, NY 10022.

HarperCollins books may be purchased for educational, business, or sales
promotional use. For information please write: Special Markets Department,
HarperCollins Publishers Inc., 10 East 53rd Street, New York, NY 10022.

FIRST EDITION

Designed by Kate Nichols

Printed on acid-free paper

Library of Congress Cataloging-in-Publication Data
Sterry, David.
    Chicken : Self-portrait of a young man for rent / David Henry Sterry.—
1st ed.
        p. cm.
    ISBN 0-06-039418-8
    1. Sterry, David. 2. Male prostitutes—California—Los Angeles—Biography.
3. Male prostitution—California—Los Angeles. 4. Teenage prostitution—
California—Los Angeles. I. Title.
HQ146.L7 S74 2002
306.74'3'0979494—dc21
                                                        2001041674

        02   03   04   05   06   RRD   10   9   8   7   6   5   4   3   2   1

7/02

*This is dedicated
to all the boys and girls who have been,
and continue to be, victims of abuse
at the hands of adults.*

Ask for help. Tell your story.

chick·en/ˈchi-kən / *n*, *slang:* a teenager who engages in indiscriminate sexual practices for money.

1. The Tall Sexy Man & the Nun

*Children begin by loving their parents,
after a time they judge them, rarely, if
ever, do they forgive them.*

—OSCAR WILDE

I wasn't molested as a child. No one beat me with a coat hanger. I was never burned by my evil baby-sitter's cigarette. I grew up in neighborhoods where kids played ball, swung on swings, and rode merry-go-rounds. Santa slid down my chimney, the Easter Bunny hid chocolate eggs in my yard, and the Tooth Fairy left a quarter under my pillow.

A rosy patina of relentless suburban niceness shimmers on the surface of my childhood: roses swimming gently in beds, summery-smelling freshly mown grass moaning, golden leaves falling like floating autumnal coins; the taste of cold watermelon and the lick of a soft cloud of ice cream cone; toboggans and hot chocolate; Fourth of July fireworks and Tom Turkey Thanksgivings; Cream of Wheat mornings and *Cat in the Hat* nights.

You were happy where I grew up, and if you weren't, you had the decency not to mention it. I don't remember ever seeing a black person, except for the maids who magically appeared in the morning to clean up after us, then disappeared on the afternoon bus.

Into this brave New World came my mother and father, English immigrants from Newcastle, land of lily-skinned, thick-skulled, black-lunged, Broon Ale–swigging Geordies, escaping a land as hard and cold as the coal you're not supposed to bring there.

My mom and dad became American citizens the instant they could, and we had a big party to celebrate, with sparklers twinkling atop a red-white-and-blue sugarlard-icing United States flag–covered cake.

My parents are in many ways embodiments of the American Dream. They came to this country with basically nothing but the clothes on their backs, and after twenty years of hard work, sweat, and sacrifice, they were getting divorced, totally broke, and deep in therapy.

On Friday afternoon in late Hollywood August, I'm seventeen-year-old freshmeat, just arrived to start my college career at Immaculate Heart College. Sister Liz, a wimply nun, checks me into school. She reminds me of the Singing Nun from my childhood. Only she doesn't sing. She tells me they don't have any dorms. I'm shocked. In exile at boarding school, I'd decided to go to college early; Immaculate Heart was the only place that would take me without a high-school diploma. Never dawned on my sixteen-year-old brain to ask for help with the application. Or, for that matter, to ask whether IHC had dorms. I didn't ask. After it was decided that I would live with

my mom in L.A., no further arrangements had seemed necessary. But things change so quickly sometimes.

I have no place to sleep. I have twenty-seven dollars. So I
call my father. He says he's having a cash-flow problem. I'm
confused. My dad lives in the large lap of luxury. He seems anxious to get me off the phone, and I can hear a woman who's not
my mother in the background.

"Whatever—" I manage to mumble. Then I hang up.

I consider calling my mom. I quickly reject the idea. The fact
that her young lover has in my mind replaced me as the man in
her life is just too much to swallow.

I ask Sister Liz if they have a place for me to crash. She says
they're not insured for student crashing, but as a last resort, if I
need a place to sleep for the night, she could possibly try to
arrange something, although she'd really prefer not to.

"Whatever—" I manage to mumble again.

I store my bags. I walk out of Immaculate Heart College,
seventeen, no place to sleep, twenty-seven dollars in my pocket,
and an angry beehive in my skull.

The weight of it sinks me to the curb, my head coming to
rest in my hands. Six months ago I was guzzling rotgut and
smoking angel wings at boarding school. Now my American
Dream family's exploded like a land mine in a bomb shelter, and
the shrapnel is flying thick and fast all around me.

IHC sits high atop a hill looking down on Hollywood, its
superstar billboards looming over thick boulevards crammed
with large cars. As a sweet breeze blows, the Lost Angel Siren
sings her beautiful melody to me, and I'm sucked toward that
voice no man can resist.

Next thing I know I'm strolling down the hill into Tinsel

Town, swallowing my pain like a poison pea pellet, and replacing it with what I intend to be a peacocky strut. I'm working hard to perfect my strut.

My hair is brown, thick, and deep, my legs have my mom's muscles, and I come with long feet and big hands, nuthugging elephantbells, a too-tight T with a Rolling Stones tongue licking the world, and red high-tops. One green sock, one blue sock.

I have no idea where I'm going, or what I'm doing, but as I bust my strut into the gut of Hollywood and float over the sidewalkstars, I feel for no reason that it's a good day to be alive, with these palm trees waving at me and the afternoon sun bathing on my face in this new place, my past back there, and my future right in front of me on the Boulevard of Dreams.

I walk all the way up Hollywood Boulevard to Grauman's Chinese Theater: past turistas snapping shots; wannabe starlets sparkling by in miniskirts with head shots in their hands and moondust in their eyes; rowdy cowboys drinking with drunken Indians; black businessmen bustling by briskly in crisp suits; ladies who do not lunch with nylons rolled up below the knee pushing shopping carts full of everything they own; Mustangs rubbing up against muscular Mercedes and Hell's Angels hogs.

It's a sick twisted Wonderland, and I'm Alice.

My mom was an emotional woman who cried at the drop of a pin. At the drop of a hat. At the drop of a hat pin. Calm ivory skin, sturdy oak hair, a grand laugh, and smart dark eyes full of love. She could make a wild wailing hard-baked baby coo with the soothe of her touch. Her father, a professional athlete and amateur pedophile, was an olive-hued man of black silences, eyes, and hair.

My dad was a chemist and mathematician, distant, intellectual, racked with silence masked by my charm and snappy patter. He was one of the fair freckled folk of the North of England. Not tall, with a bony nose, he was spindly, nimble, quick, and tricky. Dad had a big brain. He was the first in his family to go to college, unheard of for a coal miner's son. And that man could work. Work, work, work. He was wound Newcastle-coal tight to begin with, and every minute he worked he seemed to get a little tighter. But at a time when being a Provider was paramount, he was a paramount Provider. My dad had love in his heart, he just had trouble getting it out.

His brain and her heart took my mom and dad from the oothooses and Broon Ale of an English pit village to the heart of America, with a beautiful five-bedroom Spanish-style Craftsman, complete with a swimming pool, servants' quarters, and a fountain spewing pompously in the front yard.

I'm standing in front of Grauman's, smack-dab in the middle of this Hollywood Friday night, staring at Marilyn Monroe's handprints.

"Marilyn . . . now, there was a woman."

A tall black man stares at me. He's the first person I talk to in L.A. who's not a nun.

"Yeah . . . Marilyn . . ." I have no idea what I'm talking about.

"My old lady used to say she was fat, but I like a woman with an ass on her," drawls the tall black man, who wears a black shirt that says SEXY in silver sparkly letters.

"Yeah, a woman's gotta have an ass on her." I'm just trying to keep up.

"Now, Marilyn, she was a movie star. Not like these bitches today. No style. Skanky, bony-assed bitches . . ."

The tall black man with the SEXY shirt starts walking. I walk with him. Seems like the thing to do.

"Where you from?" he asks.

I don't know how to answer this question. I'm not from anywhere right now, and the panic of that punches me in the nuts. Then I remember reading in a magazine that when you feel anxious or irritated, all you have to do is change the record in your head. Replace the bad thoughts with good thoughts. So that's what I do. I change the record. I'm in Hollywood, it's packed with exciting people from all over the world, and I'm one of them.

"I said, 'Where you from?' " SEXY repeats.

"All over . . ." I'm trying to be very Whatever.

"I been there," he says.

I laugh, he laughs, then we laugh together.

"Where you live?" he asks.

"Around . . ." I attempt a world-weary smile, but it doesn't work.

"Hey, you hungry? Wanna steak?" asks SEXY.

Steak. Yes. Good. Steak. That's the best idea I've heard in a donkey's age, as my mom used to say.

He walks and I walk with him, talking about thisandthat, nothing really, just easy talk. We wander off Hollywood Boulevard onto a side street and into a stucco apartment building that at one time had probably been white but is now a beigy gray.

He leads me through a dust bowl of a lobby that smells of bad booze, soiled cigarettes, and stale cats; up a staircase where bogeymen peek out from the darkunder; and down a hall where a rotten orange of a bloodstained carpet crawls.

He opens a door and starts to lead me into a dark apartment. My mom and dad haven't anticipated me being in this kind of situation, so they haven't prepared me for it, and I follow him in without blinking or batting a lash or an eye.

If I'd been watching me in a movie I would've yelled at the screen—

"Don't go in that door!"

But I'm not watching myself in a movie, so I waltz right in. I'm really looking forward to my steak.

SEXY turns on a dim little light, and a poster of a Negrita with thigh-high boots, hothothotpants, a mushroomcloud Afro, and a mouth that promises untold excitement stares at me. *Foxy Chocolate* is the title, I think, although I can't be sure.

I sit on a sad overripe couch. It's snowing inside the television. The tall man with the SEXY shirt disappears into the kitchen. I ponder calling my father. I look around. No phone. Corpses of ancient aluminum-foil frozen dinners, cold old chicken bones, and industrial-size malt-liquor cans standing like headstones over the graves of dead beers, but no phone. I try to concentrate on the show behind the snow, where excited people are winning something from a silvertongued devil in a shiny suit whipping frenzy into a salivating studio audience.

SEXY appears with two pink steaks on two green plates.

Just two pink steaks on two green plates.

"Hunger is the best sauce," my mom used to say. I'm hungry.

The smell invades me and my carnivore growls, salivary glands pumping a rich river of digestive fluids down my throat, as I rip into the meat of it, teeth sinking in warm flesh, bloody juice flooding my tongue, hot meat sliding down my gullet.

Before I know it, only the green plate is left.

My eyelids suddenly feel like safes being thrown from a tall building. I hadn't slept much the night before. Or the night before that. I keep having nightmares.

"Wanna crash?" His tall baritone slides over me like a chocolate mousse smoothie.

Crash. Yes. Crash. Good idea. He leads me into his black bedroom. I'm asleep on my feet, shuffling toward the bed that waits to embrace me. I remove my shoes and put them at the foot of a falling-apart chair that looks like my uncle Ronnie home from a heavy night boozing. An old coat in the corner resembles a large slouching rodent. A lizard shoe flicks its tongue at me. The steak is warm and yummy, resting like a hamster in the tummy of a snake as I curl into the skank of the mattress.

I'm asleep.

I'm exiled to the Elba of boarding school for being a huge pain in the ass when I'm sixteen. I don't want to be expelled from my family, but no matter how much kick I put in my scream, my mom and dad ignore me. So I suck it up, pack up my troubles, and take it like a man.

Whatever.

As a result, I'm a little unclear exactly what happened to my happy family back in Dallas, but this much is known:

1) My mom moves her friend into my recently vacated room.
2) One afternoon thereafter, my dad comes home from his explosives plant to install a basketball hoop for my sister's birthday and discovers my mother—his wife— in his bed with her new best friend.
3) All hell breaks loose.

Red rockets rip into me, blasting a bolt of agony up my buggered guts, splitting my heart, and burying shafts of pain in my brain. I've severed ligaments, snapped ribs, shattered toes, cracked a head, and broken a nose, but I've never felt pain like that.

I can't see anything. Can't hear anything. Can't smell anything. Can't touch anything. Can't taste anything.

All there is is pain.

I try to yank away, but I can't move. I don't know how he did it, but the tall man with the SEXY shirt has gotten inside me, impossibly huge and violent, and he has me pinned, his chest pressed into my back, right arm underneath me, holding my shoulder with his hand, hot breath stenching my neck, growling into my ear like a feeding beast, punishing me with his flaming rage, tearing a hole in me.

Smell's the first sense to return, as the funk of the sour-beer old moldy body fluid mattress fills my face.

Sound's next. He's calling me a punk and a bitch and a faggot as he rapes me.

Everything slowmotions now. I pull my right arm free, ram it up hard as I can toward his face, and the hard bone of my elbow drives into the soft cartilage of his Adam's apple, a sucking pain sound jolting out of him as he yanks back, breath spasming asthmatically.

Whipping him out of me, I'm suddenly blessedly empty. I move fast now, all animal instinct, and while he wheezes from the bed, I grab my shoes, shoot from the bedroom, stumble, stub my toe on the couch. I hear my brain say, "Stubbed toe on couch," but there's no pain. I slam open the door, flash down the hall, leap three steps at a time, fly out the lobby onto the street, and hit the hot pavement running fast as I can.

Slowing slightly in the cool latenight earlymorning air, I slip into my red hightops. I do not stop to tie them.

As I speedwalk onto Hollywood Boulevard, Saturday morning's moving in on Friday night, vampyres scurrying in before the first ray of dawn turns them to dust. It smells like an ashtray. Streetlights aren't off yet, and the dark chill clings still as night tries desperately not to give up the ghost.

Clodding along over and under the fading stars, the adrenaline anesthetic begins to wear off and the pain creeps in, starting at the tip of the bottom, and pulsating an ache that shoots all the way up through me.

A thick cloud of tears appears. Everything hurts. I deserve it. But I won't cry. I don't understand how tears work yet.

I grimace as I limp gingerly, trying not to breathe too much, head down shuffling, stargazing to keep from dropping right off the face of the earth, past the hungry hookers and the horny johns who don't have enough money, the smackdaddies and the boozebabies, the clodhoppers and the pillpoppers.

Oh God, I'm so tired. I can barely keep putting one foot in front of the other. But the fear that the man with the SEXY shirt might be following spreads like a brushfire through my ass and keeps me moving at a brisk clip.

I feel wet between my legs. I reach inside my pants. Warm thick liquid pools. I pull out my hand. It's red with my blood. Looks like I killed something.

I reach into my pocket. My twenty-seven dollars is gone.

2. The Holy Poultry Grail

My bucket's got a hole in it.

—HANK WILLIAMS

Hungry.

Saturday morning is waking up, shops opening their mouths and yawning, seers of sights emerging from cheap hotels on their way to big American breakfasts.

Hungry.

Bloody and nasty, I wander like a moving violation down Hollywood Boulevard, the sun slowly exposing herself, as the smells of eggs, bacon, and pancakes start a hollow rumble in my stomach that distracts me from the pain in my ass.

A little pink peeks out from under the horizon as I pass Hollywood Fried Chicken. I can't take another step, so I lean like a broken soldier against a Dumpster in the shadow of the restaurant.

Soon as I stop, the tears are there again, close enough to drink.

I smell a greasy chicken perfume crooning from inside the Dumpster, and it lifts me right up onto my feet. I peer in and spot an almost full container of almost uneaten chicken. I reach into the Dumpster, but even on tiptoes I can't quite grab the bucket. Then the hunger hoists me up, and before I know it I'm in the Dumpster, trash swallowing my shoes, air thick with rotted coleslaw and rancid meat. As orange joins pink around the rim of Hollywood, I can't tell where the garbage ends and I begin. But there's no turning back. I can see clearly now that my future depends on reaching this holy poultry grail.

I wade through skanky refuse until finally I get there. I reach down, grab that bucket of chicken, and hold it over my head like I just won a gold medal in the Olympic Dumpster hunting event.

It's full of legs and thighs. No wings. Just legs and thighs. I take this as a good sign.

Then I can feel someone watching me. I look up. The sun blinds me with its first fullfaced appearance of the day, and the silhouette of the tall black man with the SEXY shirt appears. Oh God, he's here to rip me up again. I clench unconsciously and a mad stab of pain sears me. I sink to my knees in stinking filth, clinging to my chicken. Slowly he moves toward me, and my blood roars, drowning out all the Hollywood morning noise.

I'm going to die in this Dumpster. I know it now. A dead calm envelops me. It can't possibly be any worse than this.

My father later told me he first suspected something was hinky with my mom when he found a book in a bag she packed for a trip with her new friend she'd moved into my vacated room.

The book was called *A Woman's Orgasm,* or *Women and Their Orgasms,* or *Orgasms and Women.* Something like that.

I don't think my father was aware at the time that a woman

could actually have an orgasm, but even he knew this was not a good sign for the marriage.

Sexy steps forward and leans on the Dumpster. I see him clearly for the first time now. It's not SEXY. It's someone else. A new black man. And he's small, not tall. He's smiling. At me. With deep, teasing coffee eyes—

"Whatchew doin', boy?"

This is my problem in a nutshell. I have no idea what I'm doing. But his voice is smooth, loose, and soothing, like a lily pad floating in a warm Savannah pond. It makes everything unclench.

"You lookin' to git you some chickin?"

I swear to God he's flirting with me. I squeam. Fool me once I'm an idiot. Fool me twice I'm twice as big an idiot. I want to say something. I need to say something. But my father's jaw locks around my mouth, and it will not open.

"Git out the Dumpstah, boy, Ah'll give you some chickin." He's all mint-julep Old South Charm School charm.

I'm paralyzed, raw and sore, a wounded freak in a trash cage. God seems to be reaching His hand out to me. But what would God be doing in Hollywood? And what if it's not God at all? What if it's the Devil? Having just met the Devil, I'm terrified of the prospect of a return engagement.

"Come on, boy, git out the Dumpstah . . ."

The small sexy man clucks like a hen den mother.

Dazed and confused, I put down the chicken, hop out of the Dumpster, and brush off some scum.

"Whatchew doin' in there, boy?" Big brown doe boy eyes size me up. "You need a job?"

A job. Yes. A job. That's what I need. That's exactly what I need. Or is this small black sexy man just jacking with me so he can crack me open like a ripe melon?

"What kind of job?" I say, full of need and please.

"Fryin' chickin," he says, like, "What the hell do you expect, stupid?" Then he walks toward the back door of Hollywood Fried Chicken.

I follow three or four feet behind, wary, wounded, and feral. He takes out an oversized key ring, opens one lock, then another, then the big black back door. Then he enters.

I hover like my own ghost just outside the doorway, smelling that deep comforting chicken fry smell. He punches some numbers into a small box on the wall. If the guy has the keys and knows how to turn off the alarm, he's gotta be the manager. Right?

"Boy, don't jest stand there, come awn in."

He holds out an apron. I have to enter to take it. I enter. I take it. I put it on. Feels good to belong to something.

I have no idea what a wonderful joke the gods are playing on me. Torn apart and lost in a Dumpster, at the lowest moment in my young life, I'm brought face-to-face with the man who'll teach me all about chicken.

How to fry one. How to be one.

My dad's response to finding his goodwife cuckolding him is to buy her and her new lover a brand-new Pinto, a car offered to the public at the time by the Ford Motor Company.

However, unbeknownst to anyone, that would be the year Pintos were recalled by the Ford Motor Company, their gas tanks having a nasty habit of exploding. In addition, the doors were too heavy, so after a while the weight of them, combined with the force of gravity, made them fall quite off.

So when my mom eased out of the driveway in Dallas with her kids (minus me) and her young lover, headed for the rest of her new life, she was doing so in a time bomb with the doors falling off.

Four minutes.

That's how long it takes me to learn everything there is to know about the industrial frying of chicken.

1) Soak chicken bits in foul yellowish liquid.
2) Dump into batter.
3) Shake until fully glommed.
4) Dump batter-glommed chicken bits into industrial-strength boiling oil-filled inferno fryer.
5) Set dials.
6) Lock and load fryer.
7) When buzzer buzzes, dump deeply fried chicken bits onto tray and slide under megamagma heat lamps.

Sunny explains all this to me very slowly, like I'm a glue sniffer who just smoked angel dust. He begins going over the whole thing again, but stops and stares when he sees I'm already doing it.

In Hueytown, Alabama, when something's slightly off, people say: "Nigger in the woodshed."

Several times that day I catch Sunny slipping me some eye. He starts to say something, then backs off, chuckling. This is what it looks like he's thinking: "Nigger in the woodshed."

Frying chicken for a living is not the worst thing a person can do. Having a task is a great distraction from the searing sensation in my shredded ass, the *Where am I gonna live? Where is my next meal coming from? Why does everyone hate me?* questions.

I fry thousands of chickens and eat several hundred. The night-shift guy doesn't show, so I work a double, and by ten o'clock closing time I feel like a mutant poultry experiment gone wrong, ready to run away with the carnival and become a geek: "Step right up and see Chicken Boy! He's half human, half extra-crispy fried chicken. Ladies and gentleman, he's gonna bite his own head off!"

Even though my hair is turning into feathers, my feet into claws, my nose a beak, and I have no lips, I feel good. For the first time in a long time, I've been given a challenge to rise to. And I have risen.

After I've polished the deep fryers to within an inch of their lives, Sunny comes over, puts his arm around me like the black brother I never had, and smiles.

"You done good t'day, boy."

I have no home, no money, and I smell really bad, but when Sunny says I done good, my heart soars like the eagle.

"Where you stayin' tonight?" drawls Sunny.

Oh, shit. Sleep. Bed. Roof over head. Right. In all the excitement I've forgotten: Yet another crucial top-level executive decision faces me.

As he looks at me I quickly review my options:

A) Wander the Hollywood streets all night and hope I don't get mutilated again.

B) Find someone on the streets to take me in for the night, then bash my head and trash my ass.

C) I have absolutely no idea.

I'm forced to admit that both short- and long-term prospects do not look good.

"You ain't gotchoo no place to stay tonight, do ya, boy?" Sunny's like the lawyer who knows the answer before he asks the question.

"No, no, no . . . I'm not, you know . . . see, uh, I gotta little situation, and . . . it's not really . . . uh . . . ." The sentence gets off to a very bad start and never really recovers.

"Yeah, Ah got the picha . . ." Sunny nods. "You know what yo' problem is?"

"No . . ." I really want to know what my problem is.

"You too smart for ya own damn good." Sunny laughs. "You wanna crash to mah pad, that's cool . . ." slides out of him real easy.

I know that as far as offers go, that's as good as it's gonna get on this chicken-filled night. Waiting in the parking lot with my funked-up ass for Sunny to take me Godknowswhere and do Godknowswhat to me, I almost bolt into the starry Hollywood night. But where will I go? What will I do? My mom? Fat chance. She doesn't want me around. Bitch. Life's a bitch. I'm a bitch.

Change the record. Now.

I tail Sunny to his car, walking on cat's paws. He unearths his keys. They have a rabbit's foot on them. I breathe. Can someone with a rabbit's foot be truly evil?

Moby Dick is the name I give Sunny's car. It's a cross between a tank, a dictator's limo, and a prehistoric albino rhino. It's brand-new, and big enough to house a family of refugees. Gold spokes gold bumpers gold grille. The gearshift knob looks like a giant golden Cyclops testicle. It is a conquistador's wet dream.

Inside Sunny's combination automobile/lifestyle/movable feast, it's like I'm on a crazy movie set where everything's way too big, so the actors look teeny tiny. Barry White throbs on the wraparound stereo with his huge deep growly sexmusic. I swear it's like Barry's sweating and moaning in the car with us.

Then it hits me: How the hell can a guy who's manager of Hollywood Fried Goddam Chicken afford wheels like this?

Someone's in the woodshed.

But as soon as I focus on this paradox, a picture of my violator man flashes in my ass, and I bite my cuticle, ripping into the flesh with my teeth, pulling off a chunk of skin, my finger bleeding.

Sunny's apartment complex sits like a gray sore on the scruffy neck of Hollywood. All it needs is a searchlight and some German shepherds to make the *Stalag 17* effect complete. Sunny and I disembark from the belly of his great whale into the bowels of the building. He walks me through the concrete courtyard past the grungy fungi-filled pool, complete with its own water troll lurking in the boggy depths.

The door that Sunny throws open reads 3-D.

Perfect. Where else would Sunny live?

Suddenly I'm all clammy and slabby and crappy, and the ache of my pain screams: "Don't walk in 3-D!"

Then I have a moment of clarity. I've got no money, no place to sleep, and I don't think I can stay awake all night.

I walk in 3-D.

A fluorescent-orange couch crouches in the middle of the room, creaking like a rusty whore when Sunny plops down on it. I lower myself into a giant once-green once-overstuffed chair. It's like sitting atop an anorexic greyhound. I wonder why Sunny doesn't put plumbing and a bed in Moby Dick and live in there.

Sunny asks me if I want anything, says he's got some chicken wings in the icebox.

"If you make me look at one more piece of chicken today, I will have no choice but to kill you." I'm tired enough to actually be my real self for a second, and Sunny laughs. I breathe again.

Then he gets up and walks out of the room, leaving me alone with my worst enemy: myself.

Suddenly the savages creep in from the closets, crawl out from under the rug, and sneak in from the bathroom whispering how Sunny's gonna tie me up and make me squeal like a pig. I see me naked, my dead head resting on a pillow of my own blood.

A few weeks before I'm due to fly to Hollywood to attend Immaculate Heart College and live with my brother, my sisters, my mother, and her new lover, I call my mother to make arrangements for pickup.

She sounds off balance. Tells me she's decided to stay up in Oregon because it's so nice there. And since I'm already enrolled in college, and tuition is paid, I should just go to college in Hollywood.

The beige phone is cold and hard in my hand as my heart sinks through the rug that's being pulled out from under me.

Good luck and Godspeed.

Sunny emerges in a long shiny teal satin boxing robe, and when he sinks into the loudly complaining orange couch, he looks like a twisted little Howard Johnson's.

He carries a two-foot hollow cylindrical plastic tube, three-quarters full of water, with tubes sticking out of it, and a small bowl from a pipe attached to the side. He pulls a Baggie from his imitation wood end table, removes some green leafy substance, stuffs it snugly into the pipe bowl, and lights it, while holding one finger over a hole in the back of the cylinder. He tokes it and stokes it, and when the cylinder fills thick with smoke, Sunny removes his finger from the hole, and sucks hard, the smoke shooting Old Faithful style into his mouth, disappears into him. Then he leans back and smacks his lips, like he's savoring a fine wine, and holds his breath for a very very very very very very long time, then slowly lets the smoke roll out like tumbling dice, smiling contentedly as he passes me the smoking bazooka.

I take my suck, the smoke creeps into the cylinder, and when I uncover the hole and pull in, it sledgehammers into me. It expands inside me, like someone's blowing up a balloon inside my lungs, and when I let it out I'm totally relaxed and wildly invigorated: waterfalls, Popsicles, and plasticine porters with looking-glass ties floating right before my eyes, which go to half-mast as if the president has died inside my head. And with no effort at all a huge goofy grin blooms across my face.

"Why don't you come over here, boy, Ah got somethin' for yo' ass . . ." drawls Sunny.

So here it is. I knew it was coming, and now it's here. He's gonna try to do me.

"Okay, look . . ." I assume the chest-puffed fist-clenched

bull-monkey position. "I appreciate the job and, you know . . . everything, but . . . if you try to . . . you know . . . I'm gonna have to . . . mess you up . . . good . . ."

I'm trying to get the tough to drown out the scared-shitless, but even as it's coming out I know my attempt at badness is an extremely limp biscuit. I'm half a second from making a mad dash for the door when Sunny busts out laughing.

"Ah hope to God you don't try that mess in public, cuz that's a good way to git yourself bitchslapped, son." Sunny howls, one of those wake-up-the-neighbors bellylaughs that shakes a foundation, and of course that makes me laugh. Then the both of us are cackling like a couple of hyenas on laughing gas, and it feels like warm waves of sunshine rippling in an Indian-summer afternoon.

Sunny tells me he can fellate me better than any woman ever could. And the way he says it, it seems like it might be true. He tells me he loves boys, has loved boys since he was a boy himself. Countless women have tried to convert him. They always tell him he just never met the right girl. But he likes boys. Always has. Always will. "Unless Ah git hit by lightnin', or Jesus saves my ass, and don't think He ain't tried."

I tell Sunny I don't want him to fellate me. I ask him if I can stay there without the fellatio. He says I can. I ask him if he's gonna try fellating me while I'm asleep. He asks me if I want him fellating me while I'm asleep. I assure him that I don't. He tells me if that's the case, there will be no fellatio.

Into the night I lie with one eye open on the bony carcass of his sofa, listening for the sound of Sunny coming to splay me open as I doze in fits and starts.

When I wake up in the morning, panic swarms. Where am

I? Boarding school? No. My dad's house in Dallas? My mom and her lover's house? No. No. Desperately I try reviving my brain while I figure out my longitude and latitude.

A snore roars from the bedroom. Snore. Sunny. I'm at Sunny's. He hasn't molested me. My ass sighs. I breathe. Not easy. But at least I breathe.

For the time being.

Holding the phone, I want to pick one of the millions of thoughts racing through my brain in the single second my mother tells me she does not want me.

"Can't I come up and live with you? . . . How can you do this to me? . . . What's going on here? . . . Whataboutmewhataboutmewhataboutmewhataboutmewhataboutmewhataboutme?"

But I can't ask.

"Whatever—" I manage to mumble. It's becoming my dysfunctional mantra.

Then I hang up. The hole in my bucket is getting bigger. I'm off to Hollywood.

I register for classes: Existentialism, humanities, poetry, math for poets. A couple of fellow Immaculate Heart College dudes let me rent their living room, and I convert it into my boudoir by making walls out of some nasty roadkill carpet I find on the street.

Turns out IHC's run by radical nuns. I like the nuns. Even though they're Catholic and I'm not, they seem to hate the Church almost as much as I do. Later they'll get excommunicated, or made redundant, or whatever it's called when the pope kicks an order of nuns out of his church.

I fry boocoo buckets of chicken, and eat them by the stomachful. I don't talk to my mom. I want to, but there's a collection of stumps where I've been clearcut from her forest. I try to get money from my father. He seems uninterested. In me, or the idea of me having any of his money. So I pretend I'm uninterested in him. Seems to work better that way. I'm too lost in the Sea of Silence to tell anybody about my ass.

Sunny's much more loving to me than my mom or my dad. Of course, he does want to have sex with me. And in fairness to my folks, my dad's just been dumped for a lesbian and my mom's just been made a social outcast for becoming one.

I've been working at Hollywood Fried Chicken a few weeks now. It's closing time. I've shined the deep fryers so I can see myself in them. I don't like the way I look. Sunny walks over and stares right into me for a long time. Makes me feel uncomfortable, and I'm already greasy and queasy from all the extra-crispy I've fried and eaten.

I'm tired of eating extra-crispy. I'm tired of being broke. I'm tired of having a pain in my ass.

I'm tired.

"You ready, boy?" asks Sunny.

"Ready for what?" I ask.

"Real Money." Sunny smiles.

That week I deep-fried about a billion chickens. I made seventy-eight dollars after taxes. That's chicken scratch. In fact, the more I think about it, the more I know I'm ready for some Real Money.

Sunny tells me he's got rich, generous, horny friends. These friends, he explains, will pay good money to party with a boy like me. I can make the Real Money *and* have all the pussy I can shake a stick at. Not that I'm anxious to shake a stick at any pussy, but he certainly got my attention.

I started having sex when I was thirteen, and I took to it like a well-watered carrot in fertile earth. I'm fluent in Sex. I take direction well. I love making women feel good, and I've learned the importance of a slow hand, a sweet mouth, and paying attention.

I hear destiny calling my name.

3. My Hymen & a Wedgwood Egg

If love is the answer, could you rephrase the question?

—LILY TOMLIN

Frannie popped my professional cherry. She was my first sex job, and she turned me on to a lot of work. It's a word-of-mouth business, and between her word and my mouth, I did very well by Frannie.

Driving my motorbike down the palm tree streets that line the colossal estates, I feel right at home: an exiled caterpillar reborn a badboy butterfly. I'm rich and big in this world, an All-American success, rising from Dumpster fisher to humpster of the rich and famous.

I park my bike down the street as instructed, and steal, nerves jangling, through Frannie's reargate, past the fountain sculpture of a fat angel, and into the former servants' quarters that's now Frannie's World.

Sunny had instructed me like a black queeny 'Enry 'Iggins:

1) Don't be late.
2) Don't rip anybody off.

3) Don't speak unless spoken to.

4) Be clean.

5) Say as little as possible.

6) When in doubt say even less.

7) The customer's always right.

8) If something seems weird it probably is.

9) GET THE MONEY UP FRONT!

Sunny made me look him in the eyes and repeat: GET THE MONEY UP FRONT! He calls the customers tricks. It's my job to trick them.

Marie, a senior girl, is teaching me about the hypnotic power of cunnilingus. I'm fifteen. I'm in love with Gina, my sweet-hearted girlfriend who's finally letting me go both down on and into her. I'm also friends with Sheila, a wrong-side-of-the-tracks girl who heaps massive affection on me if I'm good to her, which is easy cuz she's funny smart and nice. I know if the girls find out about one another, the whole thing'll collapse. So I make sure they don't. I like the secret life. It makes the sex more exciting. The silence is familial and familiar.

Very soon the synapses that fire like copulation cannons during fornication become synonymous with love. Replace happiness with pleasure. The whole thing is great training for being a chicken.

I tramp up Frannie's stairs in my testicle-hugging elephant-bells and painted-on GRUNT T, hoping for the best and expecting the worst. Will I be a loverstudguy or a houseboy? There's desperation in my strut.

Entering Frannie's too-blue bedroom with the four-poster bed, stuffy flowerprint couch, and print of what I now realize was Monet's *Water Lilies*, I tremor like a scared little new boy sent to do a man's job.

Frannie's mophandle, pipecleaner, stickfigure thin. Roasted chestnut hair cut in a stylish post-pageboy. Huge ruby ringed by diamonds on her long spindle of a finger. Kindling twig arms. Perfectly manicured nails the same color as the red wine she imbibes in thin persistent sips. Designer sweatpants and over-priced sweatshirt that swallows her whole. Tony sunglasses resting on bony sandstone cheekbones. Exotic sandals engulfing emaciated X-ray toes.

Frannie's neither the nightmare nor the wet dream. She's just Frannie, perched like an anorexic bird in the plumage of her couch, motioning to the Louis Quatorze dressing table with the inlaid mirror where a crisp new hundred-dollar bill luxuriates. My heart skips rope. I try to look Bondcalmsuave as I pick it up and pocket it. It feels good hot on my thigh, a prize for the desire I arouse, cold hard cash evidence that I'm somebody cuz somebody wants to pay to have sex with me.

Frannie seems to be going through all the motions of being a rich woman, but there's something not quite all there about her. She doesn't say much. She wants me to talk. She'll hint later in our relationship that something happened to her. Something horrible and weird. Something that would make you be not quite all there.

It's a vacancy I would grow very familiar with in the world of industrial sex.

As Frannie listens to me I wonder why this pretty rich baby would hire a whore. A seventeen-year-old boy whore at that. Months later I'll ask her about the horrible weird thing she hinted at, trying to get my mind around the whole thing. She'll look at me sharply and snap, "I don't pay you for *that*!" I'll feel like dirty vermin. But I'll be a professional. I'll assassinate the part of myself that cares.

Whatever.

My mom's driving the family's faux-wood-paneled station wagon. I'm fifteen, riding shotgun. We're having a pleasant chat, about nothing really, thisandthat, just easy talk. My mother's been through quite a bit of liberation by now. Her consciousness has left the kitchen and is on its way up the stairs to the master bedroom. What it will do there is anyone's guess.

She and I are transitioning from son-husband, mother-wife, to real friends.

I don't know exactly how we got here, but we're talking about girls I've had sex with. Mom's curious, I can tell. She wants to know, in a sweet, inquisitive way, if I like it. I tell her I like it very much. I ask her if she likes it. She phumphs.

But the can of worms is open. I can see the worms wiggling around inside the can, and I'm not about to pass up this opportunity to get them out and play with them.

Frannie wants to know about all the girls I've been with: their breasts, their legs, their bottoms, their vaginas, their clitorides, how they smell, what noises they make, how they like it:

Spare no detail, and use all the naughty words. It's my theory that she really wants to be with a woman, but I'm not about to tell her that. Don't want to queer a good thing.

Frannie doesn't know my professional hymen is still intact. And I don't tell her. She instructs me to take my clothes off. Many many many times in my chicken career, women want me naked while they're fully clothed. Some people don't like being naked. I do.

When I catch myself in the mirror, seventeen-year-old hardbody stomach, pitprop legs, zero body fat, and power hands, I'm seduced by the glitter of my own flesh.

On the first day of my rookie season, Frannie gives me excruciatingly explicit directions in her droll monotone, detailing exactly what she wants me to do and how she wants me to do it. I'm ready. I was born for this work. I want to be good so bad I can taste it.

Frannie slips her slippers off, hunkers undercover, then wiggles out of her pants. Never removes her sweatshirt. She lies on her back, eyes clamped, legs closed tight, in the corpse position.

I crawl in under from the bottom of the bed, a manchild-beast creeping between her legs, the Silence like a sweet kissing cousin. Then I pleasure her as I love myself in the old-fashioned way.

Just as she ordered, to the letter.

I'm playing the part of a hundred-dollar-an-hour lover-studguy. Only after a while I'm not playing the character—I am the character. Feels good to pleasure the mysterious and rich Frannie. I do it for a very long time, whispering underbreath what a sexynaughtyfilthybaby she is.

As per her request.

"Do you and Dad ever do oral sex?" I ask.

"Oh, no . . . no, no . . ." My mom shakes her head.

"So, you've never done sixty-nine?" I ask.

She looks at me as if I'd said, "How many brillig did the flipper orangutan?"

"Do you even know what sixty-nine is?" I ask.

"No, not really," says my mom.

My mom's never been afraid to say she doesn't know, and I love that about her.

"Simultaneous oral stimulation of the genitals."

I read that somewhere.

I can see my mom putting it all together in her head like a mathematical equation. Simultaneous + Oral + Stimulation + Genitals = 69.

"Oh, no no no!" Mom's emphatic.

"Ma, you really gotta get out more, you're missing the party," I say with a smile. She gives me the smile back.

Little do we know.

Coma Girl's my nickname for Frannie. She doesn't move a muscle. Doesn't make a sound. I know she's excited because her body does all the things excited women's bodies do: the swelling, the excreting, the hardening, and the melting. But she never moves a muscle.

She touches me on the ear with a finger, the signal for me to lie on my back while she crawls up on me, chest to chest, eyes tight shut. She wriggles so she's right at the tip of me. I wrap a hand around the hard bones of her whippet-thin ribs.

Oh God, what am I doing? My power fades and I droop limply. I want to go home now. I can't do this.

Change the record, boy!

A Beverly Hills babe's paying you a hundred dollars for sex. You're the loverstudguy. A smile slides across my face, and I'm the star of my own sex movie as I hear the soundtrack in my head—

"Oh, baby . . . give it to me, you nasty little baby . . . you love it, don't you, honey? Oh, baby, baby, baby."

Suddenly the sixty-minute boy is back on the job.

Frannie grindgrindgrinds until her breath is short; then she hitches shallow gasps, followed by a couple of quick convulsions.

Then she disappears under the covers.

I'm supposed to close my eyes and count to ten. I close my eyes. One Mississippi, two Mississippi, three Mississippi . . . and when I get to ten I open my eyes. Frannie's gone. Dread and anxiety have replaced her. Soiled, unclean, and filthy, I'm overwhelmed by the need to flee. Without even washing Frannie off me, I whip on my clothes, grab the twenty-dollar tip she left beneath the Wedgwood egg, and bolt out the door, head down, guts rumbling.

I kick my bike started, and gun it too hard, trying to get the roar to drown out the voice in my head that says how nasty I am. As I slam into gear and skid away, my rape aches. I shove it all down, and store it in my meat locker so it can feed on me later as the hole in my bucket gets a little bigger.

4. Superfly & Puppylove

You can lead a whore to culture but you can't make her think.

—OSCAR WILDE

A huge billboard of the Marlboro Man roping a cow while sucking on a cigarette looms over the Hollywood Employment Agency on Sunset Boulevard. Sunny told me to show up in my GRUNT T with my nuthugging elephantbells at three o'clock on yet another perfect California Tuesday. I didn't know it at the time, but Frannie was a test for me, and this is my reward: an invitation to the Show.

I walk through the door marked HOLLYWOOD EMPLOYMENT AGENCY. It's a plain brown wrapper of an office, generic as a can of beans with BEANS printed on it. There's no art on the walls of clowns or sailboats or a kitty hanging from a limb by his paws with HANG IN THERE! written under it; no Muzak *Sound of Music;* no watercooler to schmooze around; only one nearly invisible couch with one magazine on it and one desk with one phone and one secretary, who has a face you forget even as you're looking at it.

I announce myself. I'm told to sit. No one else is in the waiting area. I pick up the magazine. It's one of those women's magazines with helpful tips on how to store leftovers and quizzes to see if you're compatible with your painintheassbastard husband. I try to read it, but I can't seem to penetrate its glossy surface.

What are you doing? Get the hell out. Now. No, man, you're the loverstudguy, you're here to get the Real Money. More pussy than you can shake a stick at. This is evil. Go call your mother and tell her you want to come home. Yeah, right. She told you to get lost, point-blank. They want to give you money for being hot. Shut the hell up and be an American.

"What do you want me to be when I grow up?" I ask my mom when I'm four. The question takes her by surprise. She stops being a housewife and thinks about it.

"I don't know," she answers.

By the time she was twenty-eight my mom had four children under the age of eight to wrangle into a smooth running unit, but every day she makes a point to spend time with each of us. They hadn't invented the phrase "quality time," but my mother was already spending it with her kids.

"What do you want me to be when I grow up?" I ask my mom again, in the great tradition of four-year-olds who've asked the same question over and over and over for thousands of years.

"I think you should do whatever makes you happy," says my mom.

Mr. Hartley has a professional tan, a gray suit, and a desk neat as an anal-retentive pin. He looks like he really could be an employment counselor. He certainly doesn't look like a chicken pimp.

"Tell me about yourself," says Mr. Hartley.

"Well . . ."

Rule number four: Say as little as possible. Just look like ya gotta big dick, boy—Sunny's voice rings in the bell jar of my head. I try to construct a well-endowed look on my face, but I'm afraid I look more constipated than hung.

". . . I go to Immaculate Heart College, and I'm a soccer player."

That's as close to large-penised as I can get.

Mr. Hartley nods his head and studies me like I'm a Negro buck for sale at a slave auction. I'm surprised he doesn't put his hands in my mouth and examine my teeth. But I don't resent being evaluated like a slab of beef; I take it as a challenge to prove I'm prime cut.

"I just want to assure you . . . that I'm extremely enthusiastic about working." I lean in and smile as I imagine having sex with Mr. Hartley's wife, and doing it better than him. "And I will do an excellent job."

Mr. Hartley's caught off guard for a second, and I can see he's the kind of guy who probably isn't very good at sex. Odd that he'd find this job for himself. But the power in the room has shifted, and I have it.

"Are there . . . any things you're . . . uncomfortable with? For example, will you . . . work with men?"

Hmm. Maybe he thinks I was flirting with him. I imagine myself with a man in my mouth. Being in a man's mouth. I'm uncomfortable.

"Well, actually, I'm not really interested in working with men," I say.

"Are you sure? Because I can get you a lot of work with men, and you wouldn't have to do anything except let them pleasure you."

Pleasure me? Doesn't sound like pleasure to me. Makes me want to fly the chicken coop.

"Hey, if you're not comfortable with that, no problem. Our policy is very strict; we don't ask anyone to do anything they're not comfortable with. We've found our clients and our customers are served better this way. So tell me what you're comfortable with."

What sexual acts am I willing to perform for money that will keep me in my comfort zone? The voice that's never wrong is screaming at me to walk and never look back. But I can't move. My brain and my legs are playing tug-of-war and my brain is winning.

"I guess the only thing I'm not comfortable with is men," somehow comes out of me.

Once I accept the fact that I'm willing to have sex for money, basically everything becomes possible, except that which is not a possibility. And the only thing that seems impossible is having some man sexing me.

"Okay, here's how it works." Mr. Hartley's all smoothed out, his engine purring. "We give you a pager. We ask that you keep the pager on you at all times, because this is a first-come, first-served business." He smiles, proud of his little joke. "When we page you, we ask that you call us back immediately. Sometimes the job'll be right away; sometimes you'll get up to a week's notice. When you call in, we give you a time, an address, a contact, a dollar amount, and any unusual details you need to know. Once you accept a job, you must perform the job. We're very strict on this point. If you accept a job and do not perform the job, you will not be called again. No drugs, no alcohol. You'll be paid in cash; the customer pays us separately. If you make arrangements with the customer for another date, you must inform us. Failure to do so will result in being immediately dropped from our client list. Is all this clear? Do you have any questions?"

I think for a minute.

"I have one question," I say. "When do I start?"

When I'm seven I enter an essay contest. The subject is "Why I Love America."

Here's what I write:

"I love America because she is the greatest country on Earth. In America you can do anything you want if you respect the law. President Johnson is a great president. Governor Wallace is a great governor and I respect him very much. I love America because everyone is free to respect one another, and any man can be the president. I respect my teachers and my parents. And I respect Alabama. And I love her, too."

Now *there's* a guy who looks like he has a huge penis. That's a look I need to cultivate, all full of I-don't-give-a-damn and look-how-big-I-am. As the secretary gives me a pager, I study the guy waiting in the waiting area of the Hollywood Employment Agency. Tight black hair, tight black skin, tight black T, tight black pants, tight black eyes. When I catch his eye I smile. He does not smile back. I make a mental note not to smile so much, because when you don't smile it makes you look like your penis is bigger.

At first the guy seems old. Hard to say how old really. Thirty. Forty. Fifty. Sixty. They're all the same age to me. The only other age I'm aware of is Really Old, and that's anyone who's about to keel over dead. But as I study him out of the corner of my eye, I realize he's not old. He's actually about my age. His oldness is coming from the inside.

"Mr. Hartley will see you now," the secretary says to him. She does not smile. He does not smile. I must stop smiling.

I watch myself studying this manchild, who must certainly be a black boy prostitute. When he stands up I'm aware for the first time that this old young fellow is at least a head taller than me. It may be my imagination, but I swear I can see his knob outlined through the too-tight pants, and I'm simultaneously filled with shock and envy.

As I watch him smooth past me with that beautiful Superfly strut, I realize I need to be like him. So easy and so hard, so hungry and so full, so hot and so cool.

I see now that my former strut was wholly inadequate. So as I walk out of the Hollywood Employment Agency, I strut a whole new strut, a pumped-up teenboy with a rocket in my pocket and a lump of coal in my chickenheart.

I'm three, and much excitement grips our house, because Guests are coming over tonight. My little brother and I are dressed up in our white starchy collary shirts, blue suspenders, clip-on ties, short knee pants, wee white kneesocks. Our hairs are combed, our faces washed, and our shoes nice and neat. My mom's hair is bigger than usual, psoriasis torching on her elbows like roadside flares at an accident. My dad's joking a mile a minute, smoke roaring from his crew cut like the factory in his head's working overtime.

I've memorized *The Music Man.* I don't know why, I just have. And now it's my turn to get up and sing it for the Guests, their big faces flooding me with warm wet heat as I sing and dance.

"Ya got trouble, folks, right here in River City with a capital T and that rhymes with P and that stands for pool—"

Word for word, note for note, just like on the record, all three-year-old Yankee Doodle Dandy, while the enormous Guests cheer, laugh, and clap, and my mom and dad shine at me in the hot spotlight of America.

I sit in Existentialism class trying to listen to Sister Tiffany explain how we're free to make our lives whatever we want them to be. She's schooling us on the myth of Sisyphus. Apparently Sisyphus did some heinous shit to the gods, so he got sentenced to pushing a big huge rock up a big huge mountain, every day for the rest of his life. Only when Sisyphus embraces the rock, becomes the rock, does this futile, pointless, punishing task become his joy.

At seventeen, I love thinking about all this. I'm bound and determined to find the joy inside my misery. But today I'm having real trouble focusing. All I can feel is that pager in my pocket, big as a garage-door opener, resting on my thigh like an invitation to hell. I want it to buzz. I hope it never buzzes.

Sister Tiffany brings me back. Incredible mind this nunbabe

has: deep honest funny. No wonder the Catholic church gave her the heave-ho.

Am I free to make my life whatever I want it to be? I feel trapped between my cock and a hard place, waiting for a date that I desperately need and feverishly fear.

Then I stare at Kristy. It helps to stare at Kristy. Kristy's small, with a little nose slotted between two big blue eyes blazing under waving brown hair. When I look at her I think, "Hey, maybe I am free after all." I tail her out of Existentialism class. She smiled at me once during class in a way I was sure meant she wanted to have sex with me. Then again, I'm beginning to think everyone wants to have sex with me.

She sits on the green lawn, throws her head back, and basks in the Hollywood sun like she's in an Impressionist painting. Maybe I can make her fall in love with me. Maybe I can move in with her. She can introduce me to her folks. I can help her have a woman's orgasm.

I stop. Breathe. If I can do this maybe I can plug up some of the holes, stop the bleeding, right the ship. As much as I needed that bucket of chicken in the Dumpster, that's how hungry I am for Kristy.

Next thing I know I'm standing over her, trying to look like a loverstudguy and not some scared-to-death dink. I smile inside my mind. Here I am, a professional sex muffin, terrified by this girl Kristy.

Suddenly she realizes someone's standing over her, staring, and when she opens her eyes she recognizes me.

A huge long instant follows in which it's unclear whether Kristy wants me, or wants me to piss off. And she seems to be enjoying it.

"Hi . . ."

Kristy finally smiles.

"Hi . . ."

I smile.

"How's it goin'?" she asks.

"I'm feeling incredibly existential." This is the first interaction I've had with a woman in a while that didn't involve a nun or a money-for-sex exchange.

"Yeah, those nuns'll kick yer ass." She grins.

"Well, if I have to get my ass kicked, I want it kicked by a nun," I say as I sit. This feels natural. I'm not thinking about my ass. Or my pager. Or my mom.

"I'm just waiting for one of 'em to actually fly into class. I'd convert right then and there, I swear to God." Kristy's definitely putting some flirty spin on the ball.

"I don't think they can actually fly without the whole wimple thing," I spin right back.

"Yeah, I think it's an aerodynamic hand-of-God situation." Kristy's so adorable. So normal. So not a freak like me.

I now move directly into the minefield in my mind. What do I do? Ask her if she wants a date? Tell her I'll give her a student discount? Suddenly this fun, sun-filled meeting of a boy and a girl becomes a war zone, and I'm staring into the barrel of my own gun. I'm stuck, struck dumb. I feel the pager cold and hard, and hear its call of the wild. I want to move into Kristy's life and bury myself there. I try to smile. It doesn't work. Then I remember I'm trying not to smile.

"I gotta . . . you know . . . go . . ."

Even as it comes out of my mouth, I know it sounds weird and evasive and not at all the sort of thing that makes a girl fall in love with a boy. I want to buy her a hot chocolate, get her a puppy, tell her who I am. I want to do anything except what I'm about to do, which is run away from this nice normal smart funny loving American girl. I finger my pager, turn my back, and walk away from Kristy.

5. Industrial
New Jersey & Georgia

*The only abnormality is the incapacity
to love.*

—ANAÏS NIN

"The mayor can go straight to hell. I mean, who does he think he is? You don't just cancel on a dinner party that's been planned for six weeks! The whole reason for the goddam party in the first place was so the mayor could meet all those boring assholes. And my husband, that painintheassbastard, you know what he said to me? He said, 'Handle it.' I'll give him something to handle, the miserable prick."

Georgia paces and smokes like a nervous chimney. Mr. Hartley told me to be here at four o'clock. I'm gonna get a hundred dollars. Plus a tip, of course. If I get the job done.

TV's on low, so you can barely hear excited people winning more money. A painting of a schooner that looks like it's from a starving-artist sale sails on the wall. An envelope on a dresser whispers my name.

Georgia lights a new cigarette off the cherry of the one she holds, while another smolders from the ashtray. I smell booze and see the tip of a bottle peeking its head out from a big handbag, like it doesn't want to miss a trick. Next to it a bit of stocking drips. A pair of neon-lime shoe twins sit side by side by the side of the bed. Georgia has ten pink piggies painted peach at the end of her fat little feet.

Okay. So she came in, took off her stockings, shoved them into the bag, then knocked back a few snorts to lube the engine, which is always smoking.

Georgia looks like she fell into a trash compactor when she was five-eight and didn't escape until she was five-foot-two. She's wearing a silky shiny neon-green knee-length skirt with a silky shiny brown blouse that's at least two sizes too big. The overall effect of Georgia is fleshy, shiny, and smoky.

I'm on the edge of the Cliffs of Hyperventilation, my mind mile-a-minuting, pulse pounding, trying to focus on my breathing. I don't know it at the time, but this turns out to be a very smart move, and when I do manage to track down my breath and force it to get regular, I immediately feel power and control. And Lord, I need power and control right now.

Frannie the Coma Girl. She loves me. Sunny told me so. I see myself in her mirror: long, muscled, and woody. I'm the sixty-minute chicken, star of my own loverstudguy movie.

Georgia motions to the envelope on the dresser. A hundred-dollar bill lives in there. I casually make it mine. Just the act of making contact with the money is a great balmy calm to me and activates the voice in my head:

"Oh, baby . . . you love it, don't you? Oh, baby, baby, baby."

An adrenaline subway rushes up me, tingly little charges that fire inside, like an addict when the score is knocking on the door. I pose by the mirror. I pose in the chair. I pose by the dresser. I shoot her with a look that has no smile in it, and when

I catch her eyeballing me, this big bossy brassy ballbusting babe blushes.

"Would you mind . . . uh . . . taking off your . . . uh . . . clothes . . ."

The power in this room has shifted, and it's intoxicating. In real life I'm so small. Here I'm so big.

Georgia wants me to tell her how pretty she is. Apparently her painintheassbastard husband never does.

"You know, as soon as I walked in, I said to myself, 'She is really pretty.' And you really are. If you were at a party and I saw you I'd definitely hit on you." I come from a long line of toads, and it flows out of me, easy as fur pie.

She eats it up with a silver spoon. Asks me to play with myself. Play. I'm struck by what an odd phrase that is. Play. Jungle gym. Teeter-totter. Barbie dolls.

So I lie on the bed, and I play. I like watching myself playing in the mirror. And I like the fact that she can't take her eyes off me, but can't look right at me, either. The air's filled with sex, and I'm the bullgooseloony chicken.

I conclude, based upon my very limited database, that women in Hollywood like to watch naked young men masturbate.

My blood is coming to a rolling boil as I play, and if I squint hard enough I can imagine this crazy baby's the beautiful minx star of my loverstudguy movie.

Georgia shuffles over awkwardly, hikes up her skirt, and kneels on the bed next to my head, a bouquet of stale cigarette and nasty booze arriving with her.

Where exactly are we going with this?

Suddenly she has one knee on either side of my head. I disappear under the bigtop tent of her green neon skirt, and I'm swallowed up in her dark suffocating circus, where the clowns are scary and the lions unchained.

As her nether underworld zooms in slow motion toward my face, the heat of Georgia blasts me like a furnace, feminine fresh chemicals burning the hairs in my nostrils. It's like a scientist who never actually smelled a woman created an aroma of what female genitals would smell like in a germ-free world. But underneath lurks something dank humid and sordid, like her vagina's been hanging out in a seedy bar. I can't breathe. I'm drowning in all this alcohol-saturated smoke-drenched genitalia.

It's all I can do not to throw her off and fly away. But I can't. The son of an immigrant is here to get the job done. And if I can walk out of this room with a hundred dollars, then at least I'm worth that.

Georgia's planted herself unmoving on my face. A joke pops into my head. As long as I've got a face, you've got a place to sit. I make a mental note to laugh about this later.

I never went through that "I hate girls" phase so many men never outgrow. I've always been attracted to girls by a force I couldn't quite control.

My girlfriend's name is Sally. I'm five. She has pretty yellow curly hair and blue blue eyes. She wears little flower dresses, a different one every day.

I'm sure she didn't know she was my girlfriend. I showed my love and devotion for her by flying on my bicycle in front of her house over and over, back and forth like some crazed mechanical duck, because I thought I looked so grown up and tough with the wind in my hair whipping so damn fast past her house.

I sometimes feel like I've spent my whole life riding my bicycle very fast in front of girls' houses, trying to get them to love me.

Cause of death: asphyxiation by vagina. That's what my death certificate is gonna say, I think, as I suffocate under Georgia. My erection left the party long ago. She hasn't really had a sexual response of any kind, and she's just been using my face as a chair for what seems like months.

I find myself questioning my career choice.

Finally I pull her skirt away from my face so I can breathe, and when I do, I see Georgia's face. It's staring off with long sad eyes. I wonder how she got this way. Georgia looks down at me. With a mouthful of vagina I ask her if she would like me to stop.

"Would you mind terribly?" she says in a soft little-girl voice I haven't heard coming out of her yet. Then I can see, for the first time, how once upon a time Georgia was beautiful. I tell her I really do think she's pretty. She smiles, sighs, climbs down off me, climbs down off the bed, and lights another cigarette.

"I've never had an orgasm."

Georgia smokes as she doesn't look at me.

I'm not quite sure what to do with this information. I've never been with someone who's paying me to discuss her orgasm issues. But I am enjoying this part of the work much better than being smothered by her toxic pillow of love.

Nakedly I stand in front of her. I put my hand on her hard stiff hair and hold it there. Reminds me of my mom's hair before she got liberated. Georgia sighs and smiles. There's something familiar about this. Makes me want to bake cookies naked with Georgia.

I pull her into me and hold her there, feeling her cheek hot against me, smelling her smoky boozy perfume. She takes a deep pull on her fag and I feel the heat of her cherry on my belly. Hope she doesn't burn me with that thing, I think, as Georgia exhales, smoke escaping like prisoners of war from a concentration camp.

"Do you want to have one?" I ask.

"Yes, I do," Georgia says.

"I can help you with that," I say.

Georgia stops smoking for a moment. She's rag limp and drained dry. I'm still naked.

"Could you really?" Georgia asks, hope and desperation dancing the cancan in her eyes.

"Sure," I say. Even as I flow with compassion and goodwill, I watch myself calculate how much I can make off this Georgia, the American Dream unfolding right in front of me. I'm making money off other people's misery.

"Maybe we could try this again next week," she says.

"Absolutely." I smile.

She smiles back, her face smooth, loose, and soothed for the first time since I've known her, which is all of about forty-five minutes.

Then something snaps—I can hear it, like a tibia cracking—and a dark thundercloud surrounds Georgia from the inside out. She grabs a cigarette quick, fires her up, and the protective layer of smog covers Georgia again like a cone of silence.

"Jesus, this day is just insane, and if my painintheassbastard husband thinks I'm gonna save his piece-of-shit dinner party, he can kiss my ass."

And on and on.

Georgia slips her neon-green shoe twins on her fat little feet and grabs her big bag. She fishes in it for quite a while before reeling out some paper money that writhes around on the hook of her hand. She forks it over midmonologue. Without looking at it, I say thank you, but I don't think she hears me. Then she shakes my hand and leaves.

After you sit on a boy's face, you shake his hand? Seems weird at first, but the more I think about it, the more I realize: That's it in a nutshell, isn't it?

I look at the bill. It's a hundred. A hundred! I open my envelope and extract my other hundred. Two hundred-dollar bills.

I stand there in this Hollywood hotel room, my mouth hanging open like a cartoon dog that's just seen Jesus turn water into a big juicy bone. Two hundred bucks for forty-five minutes of naked sex therapy, some faux cunnilingus, and a small cup of human kindness?

That's Real Money, friends.

I'm raised a little English schoolboy, please and thank you never far from my pretty little pink lips. I have an English accent until I go to first grade, at which point I drop it so fast I make my own head spin.

As a child I'm trained with ice cream. When my brother and sister and I are in the backseat of our faux-wood-paneled station wagon, creating mayhem and wreaking anarchy, after the ineffectual sweep of a hand from the front seat misses everyone, after "If you don't quit that bliddy racket I'll stop this bliddy car and you'll bliddy well walk home" has been exposed as the bluff it is, the trump card is always laid down:

"If you don't quit this instant, no Dairy Queen!"

We clam and salivate.

I scream, you scream, we all scream for ice cream.

Standing alone with my sex money, I sink. I have a flash of my mom, and I vow that if I ever see her again I'll do something very bad to her. I fondle my two hundred, and that makes it better, like a bandage on a kid's boo-boo. It's not nearly as bad as when Frannie was done with me. I'm already learning to store it away easier.

Afterward, when I'm back home, I can't figure out why I'm so horny and hungry. I call Kristy, but she's not home, and I crash down harder.

I can't stand still, so I get on my bike and the crank and rev roar up like loud growls. Suddenly I'm wandering the aisles of Hollywood Ralph's. I pick out a big day-old birthday cake with pink and blue roses growing in a snowy-white pond of sweet lard. Then I find myself grabbing an industrial-size tub of ice cream.

A spectacularly droopy fiftyish woman in an aggressive orange wig, a skintight leopard-print one-piece bodysuit covered in feline fur, accessorized by big rhinestone-festooned cat glasses—and a scab on her lip—checks me out at the checkout line. She licks her whiskers and hisses, "Go fetch me a pint of milk, I gotta bad hip. I was in *Valley of the Dolls*."

I fetch her milk. The Doll scrutinizes it brutally, then screams right in my face, "Seventy-five cents? For goddam milk? *Ha!* I can get this for a quarter. I don't want this shit. What the hell is wrong with you?"

She slams the milk into my solar plexus. Then the Doll storms out and disappears back into the Valley, while the hole in my bucket gets a little bigger. I decide to buy the milk. What's cake and ice cream without a little milk to wash it down?

HAPPY BIRTHDAY

Is written in red across the face of my day-old cake, more like a warning than a greeting. It's not my birthday. I'm not happy. A pair of baleful pale plastic anorexic ballerinas on pointe stare at me from atop the field of snowy frosting. I feel an instant, intense attraction to those two beautiful stiff long-legged dancers pirouetting yet forever motionless on this ice-berg of a cake. They have the look of Georgia sitting on my face.

When I get home to my hovel I steamshovel a mouthful of day-old cake into my face; then I cram in a bucketful of ice cream; then I guzzle a gulp of milk. Cake, ice cream, milk; cake, ice cream, milk; cake, ice cream, milk. I'm my own little assembly line, processing milky sugary goo.

The ballerinas stare up at me dolefully and plead with big sad-sack plastic eyes: "Please sir, can I have some more?"

Halfway through the cake my taste buds go on a sit-down strike, but I can't stop eating.

And then suddenly there's no cake left. Even the ballerinas are gone. I don't think I ate them, but who knows?

Then I double up with a cramp of woolly-mammoth proportions, as my body screams:

"What in God's name is wrong with you?"

Then I plunge like a deep-sea diver into the Sugar Coma

Ocean. I see the ballerinas, with their long plastic legs and sad stiff faces. They're desperate, pregnant, and virgins. They want to stay in my manger. I tell them I don't have a manger. I want to help. I just don't know how.

I lie awake with a thick layer of goop covering my mouth and throat like a mucus overcoat, a nasty black cumulonimbus cloud filling my head, and thunder clapping through the veins in my brain as a lactic sucrose hangover pulses through me.

6. Hueytown & the Black See-Through

I loved not yet, yet I loved to love, in love with loving.

—SAINT AUGUSTINE

Kristy wears quite tight blue jeans and a very loose mechanic's shirt with the name RUSTY on her Immaculate Heart College breast. There's something so unrotten about her. So un-Sunny. Kristy's what I should be doing with my life, that's clear.

Stop. Go over and talk to her, my brain screams, which jump-starts my legs, which take me to Kristy.

"Hah, Rusty! 'At radiator hose come in yet?" I smile like a cracker drawling at a crawdad hole.

She smiles. So far so good.

"Yeah, but it's gonna cost ya . . ." Is Kristy flirting with me? I think she is. Then again maybe not. It's all so confusing. That's one of the things I like about the chicken work. It's straightforward. You give me this, I give you that. Badda bing badda boom.

"So, uh, we're having a, uh . . . party . . ." I could talk all night if she was paying me for it, but when I'm doing it for me it's like eating taffy with no teeth.

"Okayyyy . . . party? When? Where? Is this an actual invitation?" Kristy's funny.

"Yeah, absolutely. Invitation, right, yes, Friday night, my house. Well, my roommate's apartment, actually, but I live there, so, yeah . . ." I can barely get it out.

"Sure." She smiles. Then she walks away.

This girl just buckles my bones. And she's coming to my party Friday night.

I'm the oldest. I was always the oldest. That's how it is when you're the oldest.

I spend my first years in New Jersey. My mother's two sisters have four kids each, just like us, and they live on a dirt road with a lake for a backyard where we spend weekends feasting at a long picnic table on cornonthecob and bangers, burgers and spotted dick, baked beans and Bless This Mess. We swim, we play ball, we have a real good time.

My mother and her two sisters are an inseparable three-headed bundle of child-rearing English immigrant Geordie lassie, finishing one another's sentences, sharing sibling secrets, and laughing in one girlie soprano.

Even their father parked darkly in the corner can't spoil it.

Not for want of trying.

"Well, David, I want to congratulate you. Our client was very pleased. She'd like to see you again. And we have another job for you, Friday night, eleven, in the Hollywood hills . . . and this's a two-hour job!" Mr. Hartley's papa proud. I *am* a lover-studguy after all.

Then it hits me. Friday. Shit. Party.

"Friday?" I don't sound all excited like I should.

"Is there a problem?" Mr. Hartley asks, surprised.

"No. Friday . . . That's . . . great. Sorry, I had, um, a thing, but I can change it. This is great. *Thanks* . . ."

"Okay, well, good. And I may have something for you Sunday, I'm just waiting for a confirmation. Any problems?" Mr. Hartley's making sure my wig is not flipping. I like Mr. Hartley. The man's a true professional. I'll never see him again, but I'll always remember that voice.

"No, no, everything's . . . great." I hear that coming out of me, but I don't feel myself saying it.

Mr. Hartley gives me the four-one-one. Then he's gone.

Shit. Friday night. Kristy, party, two-hour job.

I can hear the gods laughing in the background.

Oh, what an exciting day it is. I'm four, and my mom and dad are taking me to Yankee Stadium.

I love the Yankees as only a four-year-old can: the Mick, all power, speed, and ease; Roger Maris, the tortured dark prince; Yogi, the swami, number 8, the symbol of infinity sitting on its head; the quirky lefty Whitey Ford, with the most American name in the world—Whitey—Ford; the melancholy, hardworking black catcher Elston Howard; the goofy support group led by Moose Skowron.

Today we're going to Yankee Stadium.

Kristy's in a flower dress, with little white socks and penny loafers that have real pennies in them. Seeing her walk in my door on this Friday party night reminds me of Sally from the first grade. Makes me want to ride my bike really fast up and down in front of her house. Or maybe I should whisk her into my shithole bedroom and kiss her all over and tell her I'll quit all my crazy shit if she'll let me be hers.

This level of fantasy grips me constantly. It's like my board of directors has walked out en masse, and everyone's running around like chickens with their heads cut off.

I can't walk over to Kristy too fast, or she'll know how bad I want her. On the other hand, it's ten o'clock, and I have to leave in forty minutes for my big two-hour job, so I can't play it too cool.

"Hey, can I get you a beer, or a drink, or . . . you know, whatever?" I try not to smile, but I can't help myself.

"Oh, sure. Cup of whatever." Kristy seems to have no trouble smiling.

"I like your dress. I have one just like it in my closet." That one just eases out nicely. I have to leave in forty minutes. Everything tightens up. God, I want to kiss her.

I take her through the small hall that's crammed Paris-metro-at-rush-hour tight, and into the tiny kitchen swarming with Friday-night college party bees. I pour her a cup of punch. As the Beatles sing about Mother Mary, and words of wisdom, and times of trouble, I lead Kristy into my roommate's bedroom. It's less crowded in there, and I sure as hell don't want her to see my nasty-ass hovel.

She sips her punch.

"How's the whatever?" I ask.

"Excellent. You're not drinking?" she asks.

Seems like the perfect opportunity to feed her my lame excuse about working tonight. But that might just put the kibosh on the whole thing. Maybe I should have my thirty-eight minutes of fun and slip off into the Lone Ranger night. Thinking too much. Just say something, for God's sake.

"No, I got a thing that just . . . came up tonight."

"A thing?" She looks at me askance. "What does that mean exactly? A thing? You get more interesting all the time. What are you, a CIA operative? A heroin dealer? A hit man?"

The full irony of this will be revealed soon. Right now all I'm thinking is that this girl slays me.

"Actually it's FBI, coke, and money laundering."

"Nice." Kristy looks at me like now she really does want to know what my thing is. And I really want to spill my beans all over her. But I can't. My beans are locked tight in the cupboard, and I've misplaced the key.

"Welllll . . . ?" she asks.

If I don't give her some reasonable answer, I can forget the whole Kristy thing.

"Oh, I have to work tonight. One of the drivers is sick. I'll be done by one or so. I didn't know about it until today; somebody got sick and they asked me to cover for him."

Kristy thinks for a second, then nods. We talk easy, about nothing, really, just thisandthat. At twenty till eleven I tell her I've gotta go. I don't do it well. I want to kiss her. I think she wants me to kiss her, but I'm not sure. I'm never sure with her. I keep waiting for her to say, "Oh, just come over when you're done, I'll leave the light on."

But of course she doesn't. In the end I tell her I'll call her, and she smiles in that incredible way girls who've just become women do. After that I leave with a limp in my hump and a hitch in my giddy-up to face the piper and blow.

Entering Yankee Stadium, I quiver with a religious ecstasy of the kind I imagine a young man who grows up to be a priest feels when he first walks in the Vatican. That awe at the vastness of God and the grandeur of man. That feeling of having found something profound and beautiful to believe in.

When I rise with my mom and dad, and forty thousand other Americans, to sing the National Anthem, my dad looks down at me and smiles.

I sit behind one of the pillars in Yankee Stadium, hoping against hope that Yogi will hit a foul ball I can snag. I love peeking out from behind the pillar at all that excitement, an invisible peeping boy.

Mickey Mantle slams a home run in the ninth to win the game and does the coolest limptrot around the bases, while America goes crazy. And I go crazy with it, right next to my mom and dad.

I limp for about a month after that, trying in vain to perfect that wounded hero Mick thing.

The Hollywood sign looks close enough to touch from the deck of the house standing on stork legs anchored into the earthquaky hill. It's just before eleven Friday night, and the air weighs more than normal as a storm gathers its forces off over the ocean and heads my way. It never rains in Southern California.

I'm trying to find my breath as I wait for it to be eleven o'clock. Trying not to think about kissing Kristy. Trying to see that hundred-dollar tip Georgia gave me.

Ring the doorbell. Stick your finger out and ring the doorbell. Stick it out and ring it.

Somehow the doorbell rings.

A white-skinned freckle-filled woman with long red hair, wearing a pink kimono, answers the door. She looks me up and down like I'm a side of pork she wants to carve up. I smile. She does not smile. Stop smiling! She lets me in.

On a long brown couch sits a jet-black-haired woman wearing a blue kimono, holding a rose champagne glass. A gigantic plate-glass window stares like an unblinking Cyclops eye at the City of Angels, twinkling its billion stars. Janis Joplin's singing my favorite song. She's already dead.

Oh Lord, won't you buy me a Mercedes-Benz?

"Say hello to the boy, Baby," says the jet-black hair in the blue kimono.

"Yes, Sweety. Hello," says the redhead in pink.

"Tell him where the money is," says Sweety.

"The money's on the table." Baby points.

Two hundred-dollar bills sit butch under a fifty.

"And there's another fifty if you play your cards right."

I pocket the two-fifty. Hot hot hot.

"Tell him to put on the outfit, Baby," says Sweety.

"Put on the outfit," Baby says, handing me a sheer black see-through apron.

Okay, I can hang with that. I start to put the apron on. It's like a costume the sexy maid might wear in a wacky French farce.

Sweety and Baby whisper and giggle. My head gets red-hot, like when my dad shaved it too tight and I got sun poisoning of the scalp.

"Tell him he has to take his clothes off before he puts the apron on," Sweety says with moneyed condescension.

Baby translates.

What is it about seeing boys naked that grown women love so much? I wonder as I strip and put on the sheer black see-through French maid apron, the burn turning worse.

"Tell him to polish the silver, Baby," says Sweety.

"Polish the silver," hisses Baby.

I had imagined so many loverstudguy scenarios when I walked in here: multiple breasts; mouthwatering mouths; sixes and nines; slipping myself in willy-nilly. Polishing silver in a black see-through French maid's apron was not even close to making the list.

The customer's always right. So I stand there with my ass hanging out and I polish the silver, while out the corner of my eye I spy Sweety and Baby swallowing each other like two snakes.

"Tell the boy not to look at us, Baby." Sweety looks at me like I'm beneath scum.

"Don't look over here!" Baby snaps at me.

"I wasn't—" I start to say.

"Tell him not to talk." Sweety's from Money.

"Don't talk, just polish the silver."

Baby's cold on cold.

So I don't talk. I don't look. I polish the silver. And the thing is, the silver doesn't even need to be polished. It's so clean you could eat off it.

A Yankees game's coming on TV, and excitement bounds around the walls. I'm five. The living-room couch swallows me whole. The TV looks as big as a drive-in movie screen. The National Anthem starts playing, so when my mom and dad stand up, put their hands over their hearts, and sing the National Anthem with the crowd on the TV, I get up, put my hand over my heart, and sing.

A couple weeks later, I'm at Billy O'Connell's to watch a game with some friends. The National Anthem comes on. When I rise, put my hand over my heart, and start to sing, I'm drowned out by the roars of derisive laughter from Billy and his jackals.

I sit quick, burning, horrified at being exposed as an outsider. I never get invited back to Billy O'Connell's.

A red amoeba of hair spreads out over the blue kimono-clad lap of the jet-black-haired Sweety, who holds Baby's carrot-top in her hands between her legs, whispergasps, guiding the red head into her, left, then right, like it's her personal joystick.

I've been vacuuming a salmon carpet for about twenty years. I stare out at the storm over Hollywood. L.A.'s one big Friday-night party. There's even a party at my house—well, the place where I live—and Kristy's dancing with some Joe College guy, which is what I should be doing, as opposed to vacuuming this salmon carpet that's already cleaner than clean, while wearing a see-through black maid's apron, trying desperately not to look at Sweety and Baby giving each other women's orgasms.

I can actually smell them now, the whole room saturating with love snuff, causing severe muscle memory cramps, cuz that perfume is telling my body sex is coming, and my Pavlov dogs are panting, barking, and humping the air.

Earlier I dusted with a feather duster where there was no dust. I Windexed pristine mirrors. I scrubbed the heart of immaculate kitchen floor grout on my knees with a toothbrush, like some lame softcore Cinderfella.

It's all I can do not to walk over and try to get a guest shot in the Baby and Sweety love show. But of course I can't. I'm the houseboy, guest of honor at this week's meeting of the Man Haters' Club. I scowl as I clean, while these women feed on my misery. I want to trash the big folding Japanese screen, shatter the glass window, smash the vagina painting that's laughing at me.

You'd never guess it, but this is even more suffocating than smothering under Georgia.

Change the record, boy.

Two-fifty, more if I can just keep my shit together, for cleaning naked? Are you kidding me? Shut the hell up and vacuum.

See . . . the thing is, Kristy . . . I get paid to dress up in women's clothing and do domestic chores while my clients make mad crazy samesex love.

Focus. The big badass vacuum cleaner is state-of-the-art and has that jet engine right-before-takeoff sound. Makes me wish there was some dirt on the carpet to clean.

"Tell the boy to stop vacuuming, Baby. Tell him to turn around and show us his ass," says Sweety.

"Stop vacuuming, boy," says Baby. "Turn around and show us your ass."

I turn off the vacuum cleaner. I turn around. I show them my ass. I'm breathing, I'm not looking, but my clams are getting sweaty. Two hundred and fifty dollars. Fifty more if I'm a good boy.

I listen as they make their gaspy, slurpy, sex breath sounds. It's kind of like listening to a kinky radio play with smell-o-rama.

"Tell the boy to do the dishes, Baby," says Sweety.

"Go do the dishes, boy," says Baby.

Sweety whispers and Baby giggles while I watch myself walk

to the sink, turn on the water, soap up a brand-new scrubby-sponge, and start to wash the big pile of squeaky clean dishes.

Then it hits me. I'm pushing that big huge rock up that big huge mountain, knowing it's just gonna roll back down again. And then tomorrow I'm going to do it all over again. I'm Sisyphus, naked in a black see-through French maid's apron.

As I hold my breath, watching through the gigantic plate-glass window, an electric bucking bronco of brightwhite lightning rides right at me, thunder booms through the universe, and I really want to have sex with somebody.

7. Hardwired into Kristy

I wanna whole lotta love
I wanna whole lotta love

—LED ZEPPELIN

I'm cooking for Kristy. At her house. Baby and Sweety are a stain on the other side of the pillow now. I'm grilling onions, garlic, and Italian sausage for Kristy. I'm convinced this is what it smells like in heaven. We're talking about nothing really, just easy talk, thisandthat. It's warm and tasty in Kristy's kitchen. We're drinking some fifteen-dollar-a-bottle red wine I bought with my prostitute money. I felt like such a big boy buying it, the son of immigrants making good in this brave new world of swimming pools and movie stars. And the clerk didn't even ask for an ID, which I took as a very good sign.

The fifteen-dollar wine is making it even warmer in the kitchen. I'm going to make this girl fall in love with me, even if it kills me. I can live here. And if things get a little rough, we can borrow money from her parents, or even move in with them, God forbid; if we had to, we could. Barbecuing by the pool on Sunday afternoon. Getting some fatherly advice from her old man. "Can I call you, Dad?" "Why, sure, sonny . . ."

Kristy's wearing a Bullwinkle T. I do a wicked Bullwinkle, so I trot it out for her, that deep dumbass nasally cartoony singsong: "Hey, Rocky, watch me pull a rabbit out of my hat. Nothing up my sleeve—" (Sleeve rip) "Presto!" (*Rooooooar!*) "Oops, wrong sleeve."

Kristy lets loose a gutbusting blast of laugh that makes me believe I just might be free after all.

Candles burn. Scarves are tied around bedposts and headboard. Joan of Arc, Joni Mitchell, Billie Holiday, Eleanor Roosevelt, and Babe Didrikson are stuck on her walls hearing voices from God, fingering a guitar, moaning the blues, being the First Lady, and sinking a twenty-footer.

Ethel Merman sings on the stereo—

There's no business like show business . . .

I come home from school to find my mother stained with tears, which rain down her white-hot face. My little six-year-old heart sinks like a fat rock as she sits me down on that vast reservoir of a couch and sobs, shoulders shaking like an earthquake's cracking her dam.

We're m-m-m-moving, to Ala-b-b-b-b-bama.

Judging by her reaction, it sounds like a very bad place to be moving. I want to make everything better. I take her wet hand. Kiss her humid cheek. I'm being the best six-year-old husband I can. And learning valuable chicken skills.

So my dad hauls us all to the dark heart of the Deep South, where he runs a factory for his explosives company. Our all-

American rocketship crash-lands in Hueytown, Alabama, south of Birmingham.

I want to be an American, and in Hueytown, Alabama, circa 1965, this means being a Bear Bryant–worshiping, cross-burning, sheet-wearing, Confederacy-loving good ol' boy.

Purple flowers in a yellow vase sit on Kristy's polished mahogany dresser. "Beauty is truth, truth beauty,—that is all Ye know on earth, and all ye need to know" is calligraphed on a piece of paper stuck on her wall. John Keats, who wrote those words, died when he was twenty-six. I figure I still have a good ten years left to do something great.

I'm sitting on Kristy's bed. We're in the neighborhood of four A.M., and it's a very exciting neighborhood. She tells me about Marty, her German shepherd, who sleeps with her when she's home. I see myself in her parents' backyard playing fetch with Marty. Kristy tells me about her little sister Rhonda, who tried to commit suicide—only she wasn't really trying to kill herself, it was really just a cry for help. I see myself sitting on young Rhonda's bed, earnestly helping her overcome her depression, to the eternal gratitude of her adoring parents.

I feel like I could sit on Kristy's bed for the rest of my life listening to her talk. And she asks about my stories, so I tell her some of them, and she laughs in all the right places.

Then Kristy tells me she's tired. I don't move a muscle. She's gonna have to call AAA and have me towed out of there.

"So, uh . . . you wanna crash here?"

She's trying to sound real casual, but she doesn't sound nearly as casual as she wants to.

"Sure," I whatever, pinwheels turning cartwheels in my head.

Then Kristy disappears into the bathroom while I honey-moon swoon on her bed.

How very different from the last two times I crashed. With Sunny. With the tall man in the SEXY shirt. I see myself driving back up the hills very quietly, breaking into Baby and Sweety's house dressed in a Richard Nixon mask, and wreaking my furious vengeance upon them.

Over sixty percent of sexual abuse survivors go on to abuse someone themselves. Over ninety percent of sex workers have been sexually abused.

I shake my head. Let out some air. Maybe I really can leave all this chickenshit behind. I don't have to do it if I don't want to. I'm here now, aren't I?

Crashing with Kristy.

In the George Wallace Elementary School yard, trying not to look like my eight-year-old new-boy hands are two sizes too big, I wait for the morning bell with gobs of grade-schoolers in little Alabaman cliques, surrounded on the wallflower fringes by the fat, the hopeless, and the future millionaires.

"Where'd you get that sweater?" somebody asks Jordan Baylor, my cool cracker classmate.

"Stoled it awffa dead nigger," he drawls.

Everyone laughs.

"It's not nice to call black people niggers," I say without thinking.

"What are you, a nigger lover? Hey, nigger lover!" Jordan Baylor, the cool kid, turns on me, hissing in that Ku Klux Klan youth way.

"Hey, nigger lover!"

Everyone yells—

"NIGGER LOVER!!! NIGGER LOVER!!!"

Someone spits on me. Everyone laughs again.

I'm ashamed that I repeated what my mom told me, embarrassed and exposed as a One-of-Them. But my upper lip is trained British stiff and never quivers.

The bell rings, and everyone buzzes off into George Wallace Elementary School. I wipe the spit off. It's cold and slimy.

The next time someone asks me where I got something, I say, "Stoled it awffa dead nigger."

And everyone laughs.

"Wanna crash on the couch . . . or in here?" Kristy's light as meringue.

What kind of a question is that?

"I'll crash here, but I'm warning you, no funny business." I get the laugh. One thing about being a chicken, it makes you cool in the fray.

"That's too bad." She gives me half a smirk. "I was gonna break out the scuba gear and the chaps."

I don't volunteer that I was recently in a see-through French maid's apron situation.

Kristy wears a flannelly nightie, soft as babies, and smells of soap, lotion, and a woman's orgasm. No toxic-waste-dump smell here.

My shoes and socks are off, but my nuthugging elephant-bells and my skintight Malcolm X T are still on. She's under her yellow lamby comforter and ivory sweet sheets.

I slip under with her, and oh, it's good, baking in all that warm essence of Kristy.

"Spoon?" I whisper.

Kristy turns her back and snuggles into me. I put my arm around her middle, fit my nooks into her crannies, and my crannies into her nooks. She puts her hand on my hand on her flat belly, and I dive into the smell of her hair. This is almost better than sex.

Almost.

I try not to move. I breathe. Be still. I want to be still, so I can soak it all in, but the gravitational pull of her womb is sucking me like the tide toward her moon.

Then, through no effort on my part, I feel myself begin to inflate, until I'm stiff as a wooden Indian. Still I don't move, waiting, enjoying this kid-on-Christmas-morning feeling, separated from Kristy by one thin layer of nuthugging elephantbells and a little nightie.

Then Kristy wiggles. Not much, mind you, but it's a clear wiggle, followed by a wrapping and a squeezing.

Well, that was that, and Katie, bar the door.

Hands are on skin, T is stripped off, nuthuggers are slid out of, and after many sweet deep kisses, I'm eye to eye with the pungent glory of Kristy.

I breathe her in. I breathe her out.

In. Out. In. Out.

No chemicals here. No cigarettes, no booze, no abuse. Kristy smells like life itself. I'm lovedrunk, the tip of my tongue hardwired into her sweet center.

This is so different from working sex. That's dank dark distant and mechanical, and I have to pump myself up into a lover-studguy to do it.

Here, now, when Kristy finally lets go all over me, I feel at one with the universe. I move up the bed and take her in my arms. I don't even care if I have intercourse with her. I want to move in with her.

And now that she knows just how good I am, I'm sure it's only a matter of time before I'm having that barbecue with her parents, and throwing a bone to Marty.

8. Horse & King Dong

You who desired so much—in vain to ask—
Yet fed your hunger like an endless task.

—HART CRANE

"You're not gonna believe the shit that miserable painintheassbastard husband of mine's trying to pull. He's trying to hire his little chippy. Executive assistant—ha! Executive cocksucker more like it. If I didn't have a prenup I'd divorce that miserable prick so fast it'd make his balls spin."

Same time. Same channel. Next week. Georgia's still smoking, this time in a loose puce housedressy thing and flat black shoes.

There was no hello from Georgia. She keeps watching me, but she hasn't looked in my eyes yet, like I'm a male Medusa lovemonster you must avert your eyes from, lest you turn into a pillar of salt or stone.

As Georgia yammers, I have a flash of waking up in Kristy's bed the morning after our crashing. Suddenly the scarves looked pretentious, the pictures on the wall schoolgirlie in the worst way. In fact, in the harsh light of day the room seemed like a pampered silverspoon princess room. Bet she never fried no chicken. Bet she never put on the see-through maid's uniform and scrubbed the clean dishes. Suddenly Kristy didn't seem so hot or pretty or cute. Her nose seemed a little pinched, her lips a little thin, her ass too big, and tits too small. A hair growing out of her left breast was really starting to annoy me. I wanted to get the hell out of there as bad as if she was a trick, and when Kristy offered to make me breakfast, I almost jumped out of my skintight Malcolm X T. I was trying to be coolcalmcollected about the whole thing, but my heebies were having jeebies. I told her I couldn't have breakfast cuz I had a job interview. I had to work that night, but I'd call her when I got off; maybe we could hang out.

There was no job interview. I wasn't working that night. I was going to a party at Sunny's, a 3-D Fellini freakshow, and I was definitely not inviting Kristy.

I could feel her moving away, wondering if I'm weird damaged goods she should just cut loose now, before it's too late. Who the hell am I, anyway? Some whore. My guts tugged. Now I wanted her more than ever.

"Hey, I had a great time last night." I pulled her into me. I kissed her neck, my brain turning off and my body turning on. "You know, I was thinking, maybe *you* should be breakfast." I snapped right into Mr. Loverstudguy without even knowing it.

I fell into her bed and pulled Kristy down with me. She laughed. Now we were back on it. I kissed her lips, which were suddenly not so thin anymore, and I put my hands on her ass, which was suddenly not one bit too big. Kristy was great for breakfast. Then I pretended to make a phone call to reschedule the job interview I didn't really have, and took Kristy out to breakfast with my sexmoney. It was official. Kristy and I were a couple.

Then what am I doing here now with Georgia?

"I'm sorry, what'd you say?" I say.

"I said, I want to work on . . . that thing we talked about last week." Georgia's shy high little-girl voice sucks me back to this Hollywood hotel room, as she lights another cigarette.

I'm skeptical about Georgia ever having an orgasm. Hell, she can't even say the word. But I'm certainly willing to give it the old college try. For a hundred bucks.

"Sure." I slip her a sly smile that says if anyone can help her have one, it's me.

I can feel Georgia's gaze hot on my legs and stomach and ass. There's no sex in her glance, but she does seem very interested in looking at me, like I'm an exotic animal at the zoo.

Did I mention I'm naked again?

"Why don't you lie down on the bed?" I flip off the lights.

She gets on her back on the bed, and I put my head between her legs. This is better. I can breathe this time, which helps no matter what line of work you're in.

I take her hand, place her finger between her legs, and move it gently, trying to prime her pump. But when I move my hand away, her digit sits there like a limp fishstick.

Oh, my, this is a dry place to grow a flower of love. Gallons of water, summers of sun, and tons of shit will be required. There's a hundred-dollar bill laughing in my pocket.

It's like kissing dead flesh sprayed with Lemon Pledge. I work and I work and I work, but the jaws of life can't pry her out of the wreckage, and mouth-to-mouth is not working. Georgia's vagina has arrived DOA.

The great thing about cunnilingus as opposed to intercourse for a boy chicken is that the erection is superfluous, so the mind can wander without repercussion. So as I continue to try to resuscitate Georgia's Sleeping Beauty, I time-travel to Sunny's party. Maybe that black guy from the Hollywood Employment Agency'll be there. Maybe some crazy young girliegirl'll show me the meaning of life. Kristy's sitting at home. What would she think if she saw me here now on this bed between Georgia's legs? She'd flush me like a soiled toilet.

My dad loved smoking and taking home movies, and he did them both relentlessly. His 8mm Bell & Howell had a klieg light on top you could use to scan the exercise yard at Sing Sing, so in our home movies we squint stiff, grinning like bad TV movie-of-the-week actors trying to portray a happy family. And it's silent, so there's no chirrupy little Christmas sounds coming out of the jittery surreal family, captured like bugs in amber.

I'm four, it's Christmas morning, and the industrial-strength light is burning a hole in my little corneas as I swim in an ocean of G.I. Joes, sporting goods, and little stuffed dogs.

I spot my little Roy Rogers cowboy outfit. It gets no cooler than that for a four-year-old boy. I put on my little ten-gallon hat, slip on my little holster, and ease my guns in. Sharp I turn, a gunslinger squinting into the high-noon OK Corral Christmas morning searchlight. I draw, whipping out my six-shooter, and rapid-fire the trigger with my left palm, while aiming straight into the camera, blasting away *rat-a-tat-tat*, blazing bullets at the smoking dad behind the camera.

Bam! I'm hit, plugged with hot lead. My gun falls in slow motion, I clutch my wee breast, sway painfully, then drop, and writhe on the floor in heroic American agony.

Then my whole body goes limp. It's peaceful in the womb of

death, eyes closed to the roaring smoky spotlight. I lie there for a long time on the floor.

Dead.

"Life is so peculiar—shoo be doo-wop do wah!"

Louis Armstrong sings; the gumbo's got a big hot kick hiding in it, and they ain't nobody here but us chickens. Three-D's become my home away from home. Although what home I'm away from is unclear. Sunny's my mothersuperior fatherconfessor bigbrother. But in the back of my mind, I know he only puts up with me because I'm making him money.

He asks all about Baby and Sweety. Apparently he knows them socially, and his pink's so tickled by my tale he can't help but shout out, "Hoooo-ie! Ain't that some shit!" and a good old-fashioned *"Et toi!"*

It's fun telling my war story in this Fraternity of Freaks.

Sunny gives me the lowdown on everyone:

Dave's six-foot-two, a long, lean, gorgeous orphan who survived institutionalized sexual molestation and will service anything that moves. Actually, it doesn't have to move: If you pay Dave, he'll schtup it.

Laura's not quite five feet, not quite ninety pounds, half Cherokee, half Irish, half Swedish. I say that's one half too many. Sunny says, "You don't know Laura." She survived a mother who burned her with cigarettes, matches, candles. She hates men, hates women, and loves pain.

Cruella's six-foot-four and so black she's almost blue. She's got huge fake breasts, but everything else is real. Decked out in a sparkly evening gown with a slit that goes all the way up to there, she flashes incredible Betty Grable legs. If Betty Grable were a six-four black transsexual. She survived being found in a trash can when she was three days old. We talk about switch-hitting. Baseball, not sex. Turns out Cruella was an All-Star catcher in Little League. We make plans to take in a Dodgers game. One of my great regrets is that I never took in a Dodgers game with the cross-dressing Cruella.

Billyboy and Bobbygirl are sweet-sixteenish. They're Dixie chickens, identical-looking redheads. They survived being very successful commercial actor kids until they were thirteen, when their alcoholic father stole all their money and ran off with a model. Dad's in the process of drinking himself to death, and succeeding very well, apparently. They finish each other's sentences and are perhaps the most charming people I've ever met. They're great favorites of Sunny, as cash cows tend to be, and he treats them like long-lost inbred family. They're trying to sell a sitcom based on their life, and apparently NBC is interested.

We're one big happy nasty family, and I bask in the creepy comfort of it.

The family's on vacation in a Wild West ghost town when I'm ten. I've been looking forward to this for weeks, my mind alive with visions of Billy the Kid, Wild Bill Hickok, and Wyatt Earp, with the great Roy Rogers singing on Trigger.

But it's nothing like that. Just old dead buildings. Not wild at all. No ghosts.

My father, my brother, and my two sisters pose *American Gothic* for a family snapshot on a platform atop a scaffold the hangman used for executing cattle rustlers and low-down no-account murderous thieves and such.

I'm standing slightly apart from everyone, noose around my neck, eyes bugging and arms stiff, a goofball kid criminal being hanged to death.

I've progressed from being shot at Christmas to hanging in the Old West.

Horse is his name. He's the guy I saw in the Hollywood Employment Agency waiting room. I thought I'd see him in 3-D, and here he is. Horse. He's still tight and black, but it turns out that under all that dark ice he's like an oversized goofy twelve-year-old, telling a story, or laughing at a joke, or saying hey to a friend. Then the next second he's an old man.

Sunny introduces me to Horse. "Show the boy why they cawll ya Horse," Sunny laughs.

Horse smiles like he wants to be begged.

So Sunny begs.

"Git it out! Come on, everybody . . . It's *showtime!*"

Everyone gathers around Horse, who gets a funny crooked smile on his face with a trace of sad behind it. He likes the attention, you can tell, but at the same time I can see that he feels like a freak among freaks.

"Listen here, ya better git that badboy out, or there's gonna be trouble here ta-night!" Sunny's the ringmaster of bawdy debauchery, fueling the abused teenage hormones bouncing off the walls of 3-D.

Finally Horse unzips, fishes dramatically, and folds it out.

A baby's arm with an apple in the fist. I believe that's

Tennessee Williams, but I'm not sure. Veins bulging like a relief map of the Amazon, it must weigh thirty pounds, and it looks like it'd take all the blood in his body just to fill it up. It's a cock that could launch a thousand ships. The crowd gasps, mouths agape at the magnitude of the thing. I am floored, like when I saw the Grand Canyon for the first time.

Turns out Horse has been making money with it since he was ten years old, when his big sister charged her friends a quarter to look at it. By the time he was fourteen, that extraordinary organ was supporting his whole family. No one knows how old he is, but he makes a very good dollar.

Man, woman, doesn't make any difference—if you got coin, you can have some kind of sex with Horse. It takes a lot of money for him to actually put it in you, but you can pay to look at it, or touch it, or whatever else you want. If you pay, Horse will play.

He launches into a story about some trick who paid him three Gs to rub his thing on the guy's feet. He says it was a good business lesson, because he didn't want to do it, so he kept saying no, and the more he said no, the more money the trick offered him, until suddenly he was at three Gs, and he said yes. Turns out it was the easiest money he ever made: He rubbed it on the trick's feet for about thirty seconds, the freak cums, and that's it. He says he felt so bad taking all that money he almost gave some of it back.

Almost.

He waits a long time for the second "almost," and he gets the big laugh.

"Three grand for thirty seconds' work . . . damn, my mama'd be proud. She always said I'd make it in the white man's world."

I saw Horse years later on the box of a pornographic movie,

dressed as an old-time king surrounded by five or six very big-haired big-breasted babes staring struck dumb at his monument to manhood. He was wearing a crown, and that same sad sly crooked smile I saw that night in 3-D.

I smiled when I saw that box. There's Horse, making it in the white man's world. And the name of the movie, I believe, was *King Dong*.

Turns out Horse's real name is Gordon.

I'm nine. Lulu's our maid in Hueytown. She's a deep-black woman with a molasses heart, and a warm well of patience, good sense, and human kindness. She introduces us to the rapture of barbecued chicken, the smoldering majesty of black-eyed peas, and the soothing beauty of sweet potato pie.

Lulu brings us baked goodies that make you glad you were born, and my mom gives her clothes and books for her kids. The other families make their maids take the bus home, but my mom drives Lulu in our faux-wood-paneled station wagon.

When we cross the railroad tracks into Coon Town, as my schoolmates at George Wallace Elementary School call it, I see big huge cars parked in front of crippled shanties with FOR RENT signs on them. Looking at those beat-to-shit, ramshackle shacks, I think, "Who in their right mind would want to rent a place like that, and why is there a shiny new car in front of it?"

Row after row of busted-up hovels and barefoot chilluns running with scrawny chickens pecking in dusty front yards next to nasty-looking skinny-ribbed dogs sniffing around for something to eat. When I see footage years later of Shantytown in apartheid-era South Africa, I'm reminded of taking Lulu home to the wrong side of the tracks.

My mom loved Lulu because Lulu was a remarkable woman who was managing to thrive in a hostile environment. It never dawned on my mother to consider what color Lulu was.

Jade wears a red leather micromini and a tiny red T that stops two inches above her belly button. She wears no shoes. Her hair is long and straight and shines like midnight oil. She's little, but she takes up a lot of room dancing in the corner by herself, doing a hybrid Kabuki-geisha-hustle as Jimi Hendrix plays "Foxy Lady." She looks tough, like she doesn't need anything or anyone, but freaky, like you could ask her to blow you on the White House lawn, and if she was in the right mood she'd do it. Turns out this is very close to the truth. She materialized out of the thinnest air. I don't know anything about her, but I've already fallen deeply sweetly madly in love with her.

Kristy can't dance like that.

When Sunny witnesses my Jade swoon, he leans in way close, puts his hand on my chest above my heart, his lips sucking distance from my ear, and whispers like my guardian devil:

"Don't even think 'boutit, boy!"

"Who is she?" I'm a man hearing what he wants to hear and disregarding the rest.

"No, baby. Ah know my lips was movin', but somehow the woids didn't make it to your ears. Ah said, 'Don't. Even. Think. 'Boutit.'"

He gets his Serious Sunny face on. It's the same face he put on when he told me not to pull anything funny with the Hollywood Employment Agency, cuz they were people who would seriously kill you. Get the money up front.

"Goil messed up," Sunny says.

"We're all messed up, Sunny," I say.

"Yeah, but that goil MESSED UP!" Sunny says.

"Okay, you warned me. Now, who is she?" I am persistent and stupid holding hands.

"She Jade," says Sunny.

Jade.

With the money she's probably making and the money I'm making, we could get a bitching apartment, a nasty car, a killer Harley, and we could have crazy freaky sex every day. How cool would that be? I can see the whole thing so clearly.

Jade.

9. Jade

Love stinks.

—J. GEILS BAND

Jade's not her real name. She never tells me her real name, and I never ask. No one knows where she lives. She drives a kooky pink convertible and she never wears shoes, even in restaurants.

I'm tooling up the Pacific Coast Highway with the top down in the pink of Jade's convertible, cool seasalty air breezing our hair, the moon shining on the ocean and "Good Vibrations" washing over us from the radio.

She doesn't say anything, hasn't spoken since we left the party. The only reason I know her name's Jade is because Sunny told me so. In fact the only thing she said to me all night was "You wanna go for a ride?"

But when she did I was out the door faster than you can say, "Heel, boy!"

I caught Sunny giving me his you're-an-idiot-to-walk-out-that-door-with-that-girl look, but all I could do was shrug him a

whattayagonnado? smile as I was swept like a felled tree down
Jade's flume.

One part of me wants her to talk, wants to know how this girl
got to be Jade. But another part of me just doesn't want to hear
all her weepy stories, doesn't want to tell her mine.

Then I remember reading in a magazine that living the
High Life is just a state of mind. If you think you're living the
High Life, ipso facto, presto chango, you're living the High
Life. I have large cash money in my pocket. I'm roaring up the
Pacific Coast Highway with all this Jade. I'm living the High
Life.

But Kristy's sitting in the living room of my mind. I should
call her. I don't wanna call her. I don't need her.

I have Jade.

When I'm ten my dad pulls me aside after church one
Sunday, and there, with Jesus Christ Our Lord and Savior
nailed to the cross and bleeding for my sins right over my head,
he says, "Son, one day you'll fall in love with a nice girl, and,
well . . . you'll want to make love to her. You'll know you're in
love because your organ will become engorged with blood . . .
Your partner's whatsit will secrete a thick lubricant . . . you'll
mount her, penetrate, and thrust until you ejaculate your sper-
matozoa. The good news, son, is that if it's done properly, you
can get the whole thing over with in less than a minute!"

I'm sure that's not actually what he said, but that's what I
remember. I spend the next few years trying to figure out where
I'm gonna get a bloody organ, what I'm gonna lubricate it with,
and where I'm gonna find something from the spermatazoic era
to ejaculate.

Encased in steel and glass, I can see the Pacific Ocean waving at me all the way from Japan. I don't know whose place this is, or why Jade has the key, or even where the hell I am, for that matter, but I am living the High Life.

Jade Asian handmaiden lapdances all around me. She still hasn't spoken a word since we got here, and the more she doesn't say anything, the more normal it seems, and the more I like it. All those words. What's the point?

Jade lays out her equipment with the precision of an alchemist. Lights her candle. Lays her spike on the table. Dumps her white powder into her spoon. Floats her spoon under flame until her white powder melts into a spermy liquid. Draws clear liquid meticulously through the filter of a cigarette into her spike.

Today, kids, Mr. Wizard's gonna teach you how to shoot heroin.

Jade lifts her skirt, finds a nice spot on her bottom, slides the spike into it, and slowly pumps a river of junk into her hungry ass. Then she unplugs the spike, sets the works down on the table, and slowly the sleepy sweetness sweeps through her. Her head lollygags like a nodding bobbing head doll in the back of an old Chevy, her eyes drift off into the sunset, and she strolls off down Big Easy Street.

She looks over at me. She wants me to come over.

The lady or the tiger.

In a heroin haze Jade pulls on me, so my belt buckle ends up next to her mouth. Looking down at her, I'm struck by how exquisitely absent she is. Part of her allure is physical, certainly, but part of it comes from the fact that she is just so far away. I want to reach down inside and pull her out.

Jade makes me her human pacifier, moaning low in the back

of her throat like a big cat purring. Later I'll find out she charges a thousand dollars an hour, and for that you can do whatever you want to Jade. She could work 24/7 if she wanted, but she only calls Sunny when she wants to work. Sometimes she calls ten times in a day, sometimes once in a month.

Somebody tells me later she's from some millionaire family in the Orient. Somebody else says she's the daughter of a Yakuza hired-killer heroin dealer. Somebody tells me she's an orphan from Shaker Heights, a suburb of Cleveland, Ohio.

Jade brings me right to the edge and takes me back over and over, jacked right into my pleasure centers. Everything shuts out except Jade.

We have all our clothes on the whole time. Strange, I think, at this point in my life I work naked and have sex with my clothes on.

Jade reaches in her little bag she always carries with her, and pulls out something I can't see.

OH GOD!

It's a razor blade! I see me walking into the emergency room with my severed member in my hand. I see Sunny shaking his head, going, "Ah wahned ya, boy!"

It's not a razor blade. It's some lubey thing that makes me slip right into Jade, and she squeezes me like I'm dough she's kneading.

Jade wants me to bodyslam her. So I am her madman, and I ram her with everything I've got. Her body goes dead limp, and she makes the same animal throat noises she was making before. She's my junky Raggedy Ann and I'm her loverstudguy Andy.

Finally, when I let myself go, I shake like I'm attached to an industrial-strength paint mixer, ten-point-oh on the Richter scale, and leave my mind behind, screaming and wailing.

When I parachute back down, she's kind of whimpering. I'm proud I could rock this girl's world. Then I realize it's not a sex whimper. Jade's crying.

All of a sudden she doesn't seem like some hot mysterious flower of the East. She seems like a sad broken little heroin-addict girl. What am I doing here? What am I doing? I want to go now. I want to be in my own bed. I want to be in my own life.

Jade disengages, collapses, and lapses into a deep sleep before she even hits the pillow, like she was shot by a sniper with a silencer.

In the morning after, Jade's gone. I search the whole house for her, but Jade's gone. I have a little-boy panic, synapses twitching with the memory of searching a vacant house for my mother.

Stop. Breathe. I put together another emergency meeting of the What Am I Gonna Do? Committee and decide to call Sunny, who comes and gets me, bitching and moaning the whole time with a litany of I-told-you-so's and when-will-you-ever-listen-to-me's, essential ingredients in any humble pie.

In the future, when I yearn for her, I remind myself of the long ride back to 3-D, with that cold underneath feeling of being ditched by Jade.

10. Baba Ram Wammalammadingdong

It is not only our fate but our business to lose innocence, and once we have lost that, it is futile to attempt a picnic in Eden.

—ELIZABETH BOWEN

Laurel Canyon is an enchanted eucalyptus oasis in the middle of this Hollywood smogfarm metropolis. As I enter the log cabin house set behind a wildflower jasmine jungle, a solid block of patchouli incense musk nearly knocks me over. With driftwood tie-dye batik beanbags wind chimes macramé hanging plants and Mexican day-of-the-dead skeleton art everywhere, it looks like Woodstock exploded in Rainbow's house.

> *Driving that train, high on cocaine,*
> *Casey Jones, you better watch your speed . . .*

Jams through the room.

Rainbow has long straight gray hair, wears feather earrings and a long tie-dyed dress with a hippie happy Buddha face on it I later realize is supposed to be Jerry Garcia. No makeup. No shoes.

"Hi, come in. Want some ginseng tea?" wafts out of Rainbow.

The customer's always right. When in Rome, drink ginseng tea. While she fetches me tea, I survey lots of pots of pot plants. And cats. I count four, but I feel the presence of many more, and when I close my eyes I smell cat hanging under that pagan lovechild aroma.

"Do you dig the Dead?"

Rainbow returns with my tea in a psychedelic homemade mug with a drawing of a face I later realize is supposed to be Jerry Garcia. The tea smells too earthy and dank for drinking, but I bring the Mother Earth medicine scent up to my lips and sip.

It's good. And good for me.

She's looking at me like she expects something. Oh, yeah—do I dig the dead? I'm confused. Is this some weird necrophilia deal Mr. Hartley forgot to tell me about? Do I feel comfortable with that? Not really. No, she means Jerry Garcia's Grateful Dead. I see me digging a grave and putting a dead Jerry Garcia in it.

"Sure, I dig the Dead . . ."

I trot out my best hippieboy smile. Actually, I could care less about the Dead. Or the dead. I'm here to get paid. I look around for my envelope. No envelope. I don't like that. I'm looking for a low-maintenance score, get in, get out, badda bing badda boom.

"They're so . . . essential, don't you think?" Rainbow says in that earnest way only hippies and Christians have.

Essential? The Dead? Sure, why not? But the really essential thing is: Where the hell's my goddam money?

Relax, cowboy, you're gonna get paid, go with the flow, flowing, in the flow.

"Absolutely, yeah . . . sure . . ." I'm nowhere near the flow.

"I believe Jerry is the physical embodiment of the Godhead, don't you?" says Rainbow.

Hey, someone wants to pay me to say Jerry Garcia is the physical embodiment of the Godhead, that's Easy Money.

"Yeah, I can definitely see that . . ."

"Give me your hand," says Rainbow.

I give her the hand. She takes it.

"You have big hands," she says.

In my line of work that's a compliment.

"Thank you," I say.

She looks at me funny, like it wasn't a compliment at all, just a statement of fact. But she doesn't really seem to care, she's looking into my palm like it holds the key to the sweet mysteries of life.

GET THE MONEY UP FRONT
GET THE MONEY UP FRONT
GET THE MONEY UP FRONT

Only the newest greenhorn in Greenhornville doesn't get the money up front. This is what separates the rank amateur from the hardworking professional. You're not here to have a good time, Charlie, you're here to get paid.

But Rainbow has produced nothing, and I can tell she'd be just the sort who'd get all bent if a guy mentioned something as crass as cash.

So I sit and stew as Rainbow gazes into the crystal ball of my palm.

I'm thirteen, Newbee Newboy again. Since none of these Dallas hayseeds'll give me the time of day, I find myself staring through the window of life at the party where everyone's having a marvelous time.

In English class the teacher announces she wants to do a dramatic reenactment of *The Diary of Anne Frank,* the heart-wrenching tale of one girl's humanity shining in the face of unthinkable evil. Volunteers for acting in Teacher's pet project will get extra credit. Whoever's interested should come when school's over at three to audition.

Anne Frank don't make me no never mind, as they say in Big D. But the idea of acting in this thing sparks me. The whole rest of the day, that voice which is never wrong keeps whispering that I should show up.

At three o'clock, six of the hottiest of hottie thirteen-year-old babies in Lyndon Baines Johnson Junior High School sit in English class arguing about who's best suited to play Anne Frank, our tragic doomed heroine.

My mouth drops open. My tongue plops out. It's all I can do not to bust out laughing as I slide like a fox into the debutante chickadee henhouse.

Rainbow stares still at my palm. At this point I'm thinking she's a Charlie Manson groupie with a garrote she's gonna use to sacrifice me and the goat in the backyard.

I'm starting to have serious doubts about Rainbow. About

this whole line of work. I've got enough money. I could excuse myself like I'm going to the bathroom and walk out and just drive. Where? My mom in Oregon? Dad in Dallas? Nobody wants me. This is where the whole thing breaks down for me again. I don't tell anyone. I can't ask.

"You're a very old soul . . ." concludes Rainbow.

You said a mouthful there, sister.

". . . and you've lived many lives . . . you were an explorer and sailed all over the world . . . and you were a sultan with many women. You were a mighty warrior in battle, and you were a slave on a plantation . . ."

Rainbow looks into me like she has periscopes that go through my eyes.

That's when I notice her for the first time. In all the confusion I haven't really seen her. She has deep eyes, steel-colored with flecks of cobalt. A big Scandihoovian Bergman madly suffering but eternally hopeful face. I half expect Death to walk out of her bedroom and challenge me to a game of chess for my soul.

"You're here to learn a lesson, and I'm here to teach you . . ." says Rainbow.

Okay, it's a hot-for-hippy-teacher thing. I'm all over it. I breathe easy.

"Do you know what tantric sex is?" Rainbow asks.

I could dish some semicoherent gobbledygook about ancient mystic Asian sex, but she wants me to be the blissfully ignorant manmoonchild, so naturally I oblige.

"No, I don't . . ."

Rainbow hands me a smile, and leads me through a translucent tie-dyed cloth door into a bed with a room around it. It's the biggest bed I've ever seen. Overhead, high in the tall pointed ceiling, is a skylight, where incense curls up thick from fat Buddha bellies; candles toss soft little drops of light everywhere; elephantheaded Indian gods with massive genitalia copulate with lionheaded goddesses; statue women stare with dozens of breasts; a halfman halfbull is inside a godhead with a doghead; Japanese paintings of Jade-looking beautybabies having intercourse in every position imaginable, one leg up over an ear, the other wrapped around a head; old postcards of cherubenesque honeys Frenched and doggied; a guy goes down (or would that be up?) on himself; and a shrine of rosebudvaginas and phalluspeni smiles. Pillows and cushions plump velvety; blankets, fur, and fat cloth make me feel like a cat, and I want to roll around getting my belly stroked while nubile handmaidens feed me catnip.

A sculpture of a vagina starts talking to me: "Hi, David, welcome to the party, come on in."

And in the center of it all a big picture of a dark man with long black curly hair and brown magnets for eyes keeps staring at me. He's hard and soft at the same time. I've never seen the guy, but he looks familiar, like he's the kind of guy who could set you straight if you're floundering around. And I'm so very full of flounder presently. I make a mental note to find a wise, kind, benevolent guru teacher as soon as I leave Rainbow's. I'm still looking.

"That's Baba Ram Wammalammadingdong," says Rainbow.

I'm sure she didn't really say that, but that's what it sounds like to me, all Dr. Seussy.

"He's the master of sensual enlightenment."

That's what I wanna be when I grow up: master of sensual enlightenment.

"Sexual transcendence can only happen when the shock absorbers are open and connected to the life force that flows through all living things," says Rainbow.

Much later I realize it was my chakras that needed opening, not my shock absorbers, but at the time I could care less. I'll open my shock absorbers, my athletic supporters, my cookie jar, whatever she wants. I just need to get paid, and I need to get paid now. I'm seeking enlightenment through cold hard cash.

"Why don't we start by meditating?"

Rainbow settles into a big comfy-womfy cushy cushion cross-legged, and motions for me to do the same.

I balk. I'm naturally curious by nature, I'm very interested in the whole third-eye transcendent sex thing, and picking up some exotic kinky Eastern sex tips would be grand, but I have *got* to get my money up front.

I sigh quiet. I know for a fact it will not help us achieve harmony with the life force that flows through all living things if I tell Rainbow she needs to pay me now.

I am more than a bit dithered.

But just when things are looking their most dodgy, the gods smile upon me, and Rainbow, God love her, knows what I need and cannot ask for.

"Oh, shit, you need some bread, don't you?" she says.

I could've cried. I see this as a clear-cut sign that I'm being taken care of by something bigger than myself.

Rainbow gets out of cross-legged, rummages through an old macramé bag, and returns with four skanky twenties, a nasty ten, a funky five, four filthy ones, and a bunch of loose change, then hands me the whole kitandkaboodle.

I'm starting to dig this crazy chick. I can see her scrimping and saving to give herself a treat. Me. I'm the treat for my trick. I vow then and there to be a pot of gold for this Rainbow.

The only role that absolutely must be played by a boy is Mr. Frank, Anne's father. So by virtue of the fact that I show up, I become Mr. Frank. And in the instant I'm handed that role, I become, for better and for worse, an actor. I have no idea what the teacher's name was, or which of the adorable thirteen-year-old Dallas girls ended up playing Anne Frank, or any other character for that matter. All I know is that I'm Mr. Frank.

It's fun being Mr. Frank. But being surrounded by all those gorgeous, popular, really nice-smelling beauties is delicious. And much to my amazement, they all seem to like me now.

In the scene, Mr. Frank's supposed to celebrate. During rehearsals, Teacher keeps telling me to celebrate more, but I don't know how. We don't do much celebrating where I come from. The night before our performance I'm watching television. Herschel Bernardi does some crazy Greek dance where he throws his hands up in the air and shakes his booty. The lightbulb goes off over my head.

This is how Mr. Frank is gonna celebrate.

"The key to opening the gate that leads to the garden of earthly delights is a woman's pleasure."

Rainbow pauses to make sure I got all that.

"The key to opening the gate that leads to the garden of earthly delights is a woman's pleasure."

She looks at me for a long time, so I understand how serious this is.

So I think about it seriously. It's comforting to have someone telling me what to think about. I don't have to make any decisions, and right now, decisions are just disasters waiting to happen.

Garden of earthly delights. A woman's pleasure. A woman's orgasm. Tumblers click in my head, a lock snaps open, and I see the light. A woman's pleasure is the key to sexual ecstasy. Now that I have my money, I'm keenly interested in this whole thing.

"A man can have multiple orgasms . . . most people don't know that, but it's true. And I can show you how to do it," Rainbow says with absolute conviction.

Multiple orgasms? Hell, I have *one* and it nearly kills me. But I'm crazy curious to see if I can incorporate some clitoris into my penis.

"There's a line where your orgasm is, it's kinda like a waterfall. See, it's like you're in a beautiful warm river, and the current is pulling you along, and you're headed toward the waterfall, you're getting closer and closer . . . until you're hanging right there on the edge of the waterfall, but you're not letting yourself go over. You just get inside your own orgasm, and you can stay there as long as you want, as long as you don't release. Do you know what 'release' means?"

Yeah, I think I got the idea.

"No, what do you mean?" I ask.

"Your release is your ejaculation. So you can orgasm without ejaculating," Rainbow says carefully.

And the weird thing is, I know exactly what she means. River, waterfalls, release, the whole shebang.

"I know it sounds totally . . . far out . . . but if you can wrap your cosmic mind around this, you'll always have lots of groovy lovemaking in your life. You probably won't get it tonight, but it's something you can always practice. By yourself, with a partner, doesn't matter. In the words of Baba Ram Wammalammadingdong, 'Practice makes perfect.'"

I'm starting to like this Wammalammadingdong guy.

During our dramatic presentation of *The Diary of Anne Frank*, with all eyes upon me, I do my crazy Greek dance where I throw my hands up in the air and shake my booty. Well, the roof tears off the sucker, and that *Music Man* feeling lights me up like the Fourth of July on Christmas morning.

Somehow I've managed to transform the heartbreaking tragedy of the Franks into a showcase for my comedy stylings.

That moment turns me from an odd-duck newcomer into a dashing ladies' boy.

And I owe it all to Anne Frank, martyr and symbol of all that is good in human beings.

"Wow, that sounds . . . far out." I've never said "far out" before or since, but Rainbow eats it up like wavy gravy with a tie-dyed spoon.

She takes off her robe. She's the only sexwork customer I ever have who takes off her clothes while I still have mine on. And for an old broad (again with the proviso that anyone over the age of twenty-five is old) she's got a rip-roaring body. Supple muscles firm lithe and graceful, breasts slung low, with big brown nipples in the middle. I make a mental note that as far as books go, don't judge them by their covers.

I now become aware that Rainbow's posing for me. Not vulgar or ostentatious. Subtle and proud. She seems to be one of those rare people who's actually comfortable with her own naked body.

"You have a beautiful body . . ." I would've said it whether it was true or not, but in this case it is true, which does makes it easier.

She likes it. She's not desperate like Georgia or Franny, but she likes it.

"Do you want me to take my clothes off?" Just trying to keep the customer satisfied.

"Do whatever makes you happy," says Rainbow.

Wow. Whatever makes me happy. No one says that to me in real life, never mind when I'm chickening.

Seems like if you're gonna learn to orgasm without ejaculating, you should be naked. So I take off my clothes. Rainbow sits opposite me cross-legged on that continent of a bed. I try, but I just can't get the cross-legged thing going. My grandfather's coalminer soccerplaying legs are just too unyielding. I'm tugging and pulling, cuz I'm trying to suck it up and play through the pain, but damn, this shit hurts.

"Don't do it if it hurts. Don't do anything that hurts . . ." Rainbow flows. You gotta hand it to the hippies, when it comes to peace and love and all that business, they really know their shit.

Rainbow shows me how to deepbreathe, and we deepbreathe until we feel the life force flowing through us. I don't actually feel the life force flowing through me as such, but she does, and that's good enough for me. The crumpled bills in my pocket are filling me with the life force.

Rainbow and I *ohhhhhhhhhhhhhhhmmmm* for about a fortnight. Eventually I do feel a little light-headed, like when I first smoked a cigarette. But, hey, if she wants to pay me to breathe and say om, that's rolling off a log for a chicken.

Finally when Rainbow is om'd out, she takes my hand, places it on her breast, looks me in the eyes, and with a hypnotic smile shows me how to roll that mammoth mammarian poolcue tip between my thumb and forefinger, and it gets bigger and tighter, until it feels like it's ready to pop, while she makes air-suck sounds of pleasure.

I can smell her now, Rainbowing as she makes my hand the axis between her legs around which she gyrates, nestling my head into her neck and whispering, "Kiss me soft . . ."

I eat her neck like a fruitcake while she revs in growly moans, everything moving in rhythm like a well-oiled sex machine, the fur blanket softly soft as she guides me like an air-traffic controller. Then Rainbow replaces my hand with my mouth and she huffs and she puffs like she's gonna blow the house down, jimjamming and earthquakeshaking.

I smile inside. I'm getting a crash course in the fine art of a woman's orgasm, and I'm getting paid for it. America—what a country!

"Now I'm right there," she pants, ". . . if I let myself, I'd go right over the waterfall . . . but . . . I'm . . . not . . . I'm gonna stay . . . right here and let the . . . waves roll through me . . . there's one . . . slow down . . . Stop!" Rainbow squeezes, fists clenching and unclenching like a baby breastfeeding, ". . . now slow . . . there's another one . . . ohhhhhhhhhhhhhhhhhhhhhhh-hhhhhhhhhh . . . God . . ."

Rainbow lets rip with a top-of-the-lungs scream. A huge lit-tle death. When she collapses at the tip of my tongue, I understand for the first time what they're talking about, as time warps, Einstein smiling somewhere, eternity in a second, infinity in a grain of sand.

I think of busting my ass in the grease of HFC. I think of my father slaving away at the explosives plant. I think about my grandfather shoveling coal down the mine. I won't be getting black lung disease from this. If having sex for money was always this good, I'd still be a hooker.

When I'm eleven, Alabama is ranked fiftieth in the nation in education. My mom becomes so desperate she decides to enroll me and my brother in the best school in Alabama. The oxymoronicality of this is lost on no one. The only rub is that we have to pass the extremely rigorous entrance exam. My folks promise that if we pass the test, we can have some cool thing of our choice. My brother wants a wide handlebar bananaseat Stingray, the coolest bike on the planet. I want a brand-new set of golf clubs. I like how shiny they look in the sporting-goods store.

Tense anticipation grips our house in the days leading up to The Test. Are we good enough to rub elbows with the crème de la crème of Hueytown, America?

The extremely rigorous test takes all day. It's rough terrain and grueling, but we've been trained well. Not just in facts and figures, but in succeeding American style, while failure breathes hot on your neck and those around you wither. It takes a week to get the results back. Longest week of my life.

We pass the test. There is much rejoicing.

Unfortunately, that summer my dad gets transferred, so we can't attend the best school in Alabama. But my mom and dad make good. They get my brother his cool wide-handlebarred Stingray with the big bananaseat, and they get me my shiny new golf clubs.

Rainbow gets out of the river and dries off on the sunny shore, while I stand next to her, nakedly rolling my big huge rock up my big huge mountain.

After a brief intermission, Act II begins. She pulls me into the river, takes me right to the edge of the waterfall, and then stops. The most important thing, she says, is to turn off your mind, and feel your body. You can't think and swim at the same time.

Once a man plunges over the waterfall in his barrel, of course, it's all over for him. For a while at least. So you have to be very careful and really pay attention. I practice getting right on the edge and just sticking there. And it's good. When she does something particularly compelling, I feel the spray in my face and the pull of the fall, and by God, quivers do quiver me, then I quickly pull myself back.

Rainbow's my Seeing Eye sexdog.

"Wow, that was groovy . . ." I say, when it's clear we're done.

Groovy? I can't believe that came out of my mouth, but as usual I've ceased to exist in my need to please.

I don't know what to do now. Should I hang out? Are we friends? I think for a minute. I still don't feel that creeping mudslide of depression I always get after I chicken. I'm just a little confused, that's all. But looking around, I can see myself moving right in here and being the sextoy for all of Rainbow's old greatbodied freakyhippie babies. Sounds like fun, I think, as I grab at another salvation flotation device.

"I have something for you . . ." Rainbow's sweet as you please, slipping on an old soft tie-dyed robe. I follow at her heels like a naked chickenpuppy. She reaches in a drawer and I'm expecting a nice fat juicy tip. Twenty, maybe fifty. Instead Rainbow pulls out a feather.

A feather.

"It's an earring," says Rainbow.

I have to work hard not to show how totally disgusted I am as I take out the rhinestone in my ear and replace it with the feather. I look in the mirror. To my amazement, I actually like the way it looks. Kind of tribal. Even though I silently scoff when she presents it to me, I wear that feather for many years.

And whenever I do, I think of Rainbow.

She kisses me on both cheeks. She thanks me. I thank her. She doesn't say we should get together again soon, or that we should stay in touch. I love that. I did what I came to do, we both got what we wanted, and that, as they say, is that.

Rainbow's the only trick I ever had who didn't use me as the trigger point for venting venom.

Motorcycling away from Rainbow, I'm high on sex and money, floating on my feather earring in the sweetness of the cool Laurel Canyon night.

Then this thought pops center stage on my brain:

"Hey, this is a really cool way to make a living."

And the instant that thought appears, the life starts to kill me.

11. I Love You, Mommy

And sex and sex and sex and sex
. . . I'm shattered

— JAGGER & RICHARDS

The beginning of the end comes innocently enough. Just a normal job on a normal day in the life of a normal seventeen-year-old boy hooker.

Tooling through a trendy treed Pacific Palisades neighborhood chockablock with brown migrating workers mowing green lawns, pink children throwing red balls, and white women driving overpriced foreign automobiles, I have that wonderful sense of déjà vu all over again as I go from the seedy pit of Hollywood to the clean hightone America of my youth.

It's just before seven o'clock on Monday evening. This in itself is troubling. Who the hell orders a chicken at seven o'clock on Monday? It's always midnights or matinees. So I'm a tad suspicious to begin with, but what the hell, I'm a trained professional, and there's nothing in this luxurious Mediterranean four-bedroom two-and-a-half-bath extravaganza I can't handle. Dish it out. Bring it on.

Whatever.

I ring the bell. Split a second and that's how long it takes a postmodern June Cleaver to pull the door open too fast, say hello too hard, and lead me into her too-tastefully-decorated home.

She does look good for an old broad, except for all the cakey makeup. Brownish hair slicked back anorexic ballerina style, eyes drowning in pools of blue eye shadow, she's working a creamy calf-length sleeveless dress, plain white flats, and pearls. God love her, she put the pearls on for her chicken.

The kitchen's full of wallpaper choking on flowers. Linoleum rides the floor, Wedgwood watches from running boards, and a desert island sits arid with a butcher-block cutting board sinking in its middle.

It's like a movie set of a perfect American home, with a housewife played by an actress who looks right for the role but is just a little too stiff.

"Did anyone see you come in?" There's a disturbing urgency in the lines fraying around the edges of her eyes and the veins popping on her neck.

Then she realizes how harsh she sounded and tries to pretend she's all casual and carefree. "Not that it really matters, but you know how people talk."

This bundle of too-tightly-tied wires tries to smile. But there's no smile there. Then her pupils start darting back and forth like someone who's about to flunk a lie-detector test.

"And if anyone asks, maybe you could say you're a high-school student who's here to help me organize my miniatures. I collect miniatures. Would you like to see them?"

My Spider senses are tingling, but my pokerface is firmly in place. Maybe she's just a little nervous. Family's out of town, looking for a little fun. Maybe she's never had sex with anyone besides her painintheassbastard husband. Maybe she just wants me to get nekked and tell her how hot she is.

Maybe.

This home movie's in the backyard, and you can practically hear the green of the grass and smell the birdies chirruping. I'm six, and my mom stands about twenty feet in front of me holding a baseball. My bat is in the cocked-and-ready position, and I'm pure intention, staring that ball down. When Mom lobs in the ball, my eyes get big and hungry, like a lion spotting a sick wildebeest.

I attack the ball with a vicious compact swing, and when my bat whacks it square on the sweet G spot, that ball flies like a human cannonball out of frame.

I drop the bat and my little legs churn me hard to first, whip me around second, fly me by third, flushed and radiant. I slide.

I'm safe at home.

"I mean, I'm sure people have better things to do than stare at my back door. But let's say they were walking the dog, people like to walk their dogs, well, I suppose they have to, but the point is they *could* see you, and if they did, I just want us to be on the same page, you see what I mean?"

I follow my seven o'clock Monday trick to the Miniature Room, and as she finishes her monologue she opens a door, revealing a room exploding with teeny-tiny miniatures: little geldings with no little balls; tiny Chinese potentates and French diplomats; gnomes, sprites, and fairies; a very small Dorothy Gale from Kansas with her itty-bitty ruby slippers and her wee dog Toto; diminutive Bob's Big Boy, the Michelin Man, and the Sta-Puf Marshmallow Man; minute Benjamin Franklin, Genghis Khan, and even a mini–Marilyn Monroe, trying to hold her skirt down while the wind threatens to expose her panties for all eternity.

My seven o'clock Monday trick tries to smile again. She comes a little closer this time but still hasn't hit it.

"Wow . . . this is really . . . incredible."

I *say* incredible like it's a good thing, whereas I *mean* incredible like it's a very scary thing. Everything's all lined up too perfectly, there's too much of it, and it's way too small. The whole thing makes me want to run, not walk, as fast as I can away from this woman.

But I don't. I can't.

"Thank you very much, it's taken a long time to collect, as you can imagine, and I'm . . ."

Her mouth is open, but nothing's coming out of this pearly woman standing in front of her collection of three-inch animals, movie characters, and famous historical figures.

My father was a superb English footballer and cricketer, with an excellent googly ball and a real nose for goal. But my dad took up a whole new game he knew nothing about, just so he could play baseball with his American son.

The rhythm of playing catch is so soothing, the leathery smell, the hard of the ball, the red raised stitches, the pounding into the mitt, throwing to a perfect point, learning to make it dip, spin, and curve.

Baseball's the only language my dad can speak with me, but he speaks it well.

The better I play, the more he seems to love me, so I practice, trying to be the lovable boy.

"I love Marilyn . . . she was a real movie star," I say.

So we're back to Marilyn.

My pearly trick stares at me, a plaster-of-paris mask of a normal person fixed on her face. I don't know what to do. I gotta do something. Try to start the sex? I'm afraid if I touch her she'll shatter into a million pieces. And where's my stinking money? This is getting ridiculous. I'm gonna have to talk to Mr. Hartley about this shit, cuz I need my money in plain sight when I walk in the door, no questions asked.

"And she's so . . . *small* . . ." I say, trying desperately to fill in the Silence.

As soon as she hears the word "small," my pearly trick comes back to life, like some perfect robot replica of a human that gets activated by flipping a switch on the back of her head.

"Yes, they're so small, aren't they? I love how small they all are. I'll show you my favorite," she says.

I still don't know her name, or what the hell she wants, and I still DO NOT HAVE MY MONEY UP FRONT, but at least she's not acting like the walking dead anymore. She picks up a miniature with a rose complexion and dark hair, dressed very Civil War. Vaguely resembles Scarlett O'Hara.

"It's Scarlett O'Hara. Don't you just love her?" She stares rapturously at the lifeless Scarlett O'Hara doll like it's a three-inch lover.

"Yeah, I loved how she made that dress out of the curtains . . ." Having noticed that the mini-Scarlett's wearing the curtaindress, I feel this might help move us along.

"Oh, gosh," she says, "I love that scene where Mammy sews the dress, and she grumbles the whole time. Oh, that Mammy, she's such a character . . . and Scarlet puts on the dress, and of course she looks fabulous, and she goes to see Rhett in prison, and pretends like everything's okay, but he sees right through her. Oh, that Rhett, he's such a scalawag . . . and does he give her a tongue-lashing. See, the thing people don't realize is that they were always madly in love with each other, but never at the same time . . ."

And with that, she clicks into some other time zone, where crazed assassins lurk in every church tower, puts the little Scarlett carefully back in its place between President Abraham Lincoln and General Robert E. Lee, and ushers me out posthaste.

Suddenly the forecast has gone from mostly sunny to severe storm warnings. Her skeletal structure visibly stiffens, skin tightening and lips constricting. For a second I think it's me. I see her on the phone with Mr. Hartley, who calls Sunny, who chucks me back in the Dumpster.

I need my money.

I need my money.

I need my money.

So I become a boywonder baseball player. In all my team photos, with those rows of hopeful, glum, big-eared, goofy, shy, uncertain, beaming-with-confidence lads, I'm always on the bottom row, kneeling, smiling peacefully, like a little ballplaying boy Buddha.

I play on All-Star teams with all the best players. The All-Star pictures are different from the average, everyday team photos. The All-Stars are cocksure, aggressive, and cunning, while the regular teams are more about being fat or uncomfortable or not quite sure what you're there for.

Being an All-Star Little Leaguer is excellent chicken training: the same performing adrenaline rush, the same illusion that attention equals love. Reminds me of Sunny's team of chickens. Only those players end up arrested, addicted, or dead, instead of on the cover of a Wheaties box.

My pearly trick mutters underbreath as I pad down the hall after her. The only words I can make out are "ashamed," "irresponsible," and "neglect." I'm sure I'm not supposed to respond. In fact, I'm sure she's not even aware she's vocalizing at this almost intelligible level.

She stops, turns suddenly, and tries to smile again. Again she fails. She looks down, regroups, and looks toward me, but not at me.

"My husband is not . . . with us . . ."

Euphemism for "dead," I'm assuming, although for all I know he could be away on a golf junket.

"I thought you should know. I mean, I didn't want you to think . . ."

Who the hell cares what I think? I'm the whore houseboy, remember? And she doesn't want me to think what? That she's immoral? Unfaithful? Or just out of her mind?

"He took his own life. After our son died . . ."

"Oh . . . I'm really . . . sorry." I put on a sad but understanding face.

"We had a wonderful marriage. He was very handsome and attentive. My therapist said I should date again, that it would help me . . . get over the whole thing."

I doubt this is the kind of date he had in mind.

"Everyone says I should sell the house, but I don't want to sell the house. I love this house . . . Would *you* sell the house?"

Now she's asking the boy hooker for real-estate advice. "No, I think it's a great house. I thought that when I came in—I thought, 'This is a *great* house.'"

"It is, isn't it? That's what I'm gonna tell people. I'll just say, 'It's a great house . . .' My husband loved this house. He took his own life, did I tell you that?"

Yes, you did mention that.

"You'll have to forgive me, I've been very . . . forgetful lately. The fact is, he really never got over Braddy's passing. Braddy was our son . . . our only child. It was a terrible tragedy . . . his friend had been drinking . . . Braddy wasn't drinking, the coroner confirmed that. He had no alcohol in his system, or very little alcohol. They ran head-on into a bus . . . just like that . . . alive one second, dead the next. Makes you think, doesn't it?"

Yes, it certainly does.

"Yes, it certainly does," I say.

She looks at me like she's coming out of a coma, and for the first time I see who she was before all this shit happened: a beautiful wifemommy living large with the handsome husband, the cute kid, and the great house. Like my mom. Only this one didn't leave her life and make a new one; she had hers yanked out from under her, and she has no idea what to do about it.

"You'll have to excuse me . . . I, uh, haven't been myself lately . . ."

I feel for her. Dead son. Husband offs himself. I want to take her in my arms, rock the sad right out of her, and tell her everything's gonna be okay.

But I don't. I can't.

A sincere "I'm sorry" is all I can manage.

What a couple of funked-up ducks we are, this ex-mom slash ex-wife and I, trying to get some love in the worst way.

"Thanks," she says.

She tries to smile again and this time it actually works. And when the smile finally does arrive it's very sweet, and drenched in sorrow, like cherries jubilee just about to be lit on fire.

I have a Little League game tonight. When I'm ten I love playing, love being an All-Star. But as much as I love baseball games, I love night games best of all, because I get to play under the lights. Makes me feel like I'm half a step from Yankee Stadium, playing with Yogi, Mick, and the Moose.

But the afternoon sky looks like an old bruise, and a bull-whip wind whips into the flesh of the earth. I keep sneaking peeks outside, and every time I do, my little heart sinks like a grape in warm Jell-O.

Still, I slip on my white sanitary socks, slide my little blue stirrups over them, then my gray flannel pantaloons with blue pipes up the side, my blue-sleeved undershirt, gray uniform top with blue PIRATES on the front, then pull on my blue cap with P in the middle, and yank on my black cleats.

I rub mink oil lovingly into my glove, leather scratch-and-sniffing all over me, the glove molding further into the shape of my hand.

At six o'clock my mom asks my dad if maybe he shouldn't take me to the game, what with the storm and all.

He doesn't answer her. He gets in the car, I get in with him, and he starts driving me to my game.

Boy!

Screams the room my pearly trick leads me into: pennants, trophies, posters of ballplayers, old caramel-colored baseball mitt with scuffed ball sitting in it, pictures of a brown-haired dimply boy growing up cute: grade school, Little League team, camp friends, high-school-tuxed, and posing with a pretty young polyester-plaid baby.

The room soothes me like a binkie.

But the longer I stand there, the more wigged I get. We definitely have something in the woodshed here. This isn't a boy's room anymore. It's a museum of a boy's room. This room is dead.

"This is Braddy's room. His real name was Bradley, but he could only say Braddy when he was a baby, and I guess it just stuck. He wanted to go to UCLA; that was his dream. And he was a very good athlete. Golf, tennis, baseball. Are you an athlete?" she asks with great expectations.

Doesn't take a rocket surgeon to figure out the answer to that one.

"Yes, I am."

"It was his friend Aaron . . . I never liked that boy; he was a very bad influence. I tried to tell Braddy, but he was stubborn, just like his dad. There was no alcohol found in Braddy. Or very little alcohol . . . very little alcohol . . ."

I want to get out of this dead boy's room.

I want to get paid.

I want.

"Would you . . . do me a favor?" She's filled with hesitation.

I still don't think she fully understands the nature of our transaction. That's what I'm here for. She gives me money. I do her favors.

"Sure," I say.

"Uh . . . would you mind . . . uh . . . putting these on?"

Pearly mommy pulls a Hawaiian shirt and khaki shorts from the closet. I see Braddy behind her on the wall in a blown-up framed picture, dressed in the same Hawaiian shirt and khaki shorts.

I'm betting it was his favorite outfit.

"This was his favorite outfit. We used to kid him that it was his uniform. I washed it and washed it afterward to get all . . . you know . . . the stains out. It wasn't easy, believe you me, but I've always said if you want something bad enough and you're willing to work at it, you can accomplish anything. Don't you think?"

"Definitely . . ." I say.

"Would you mind?" She hands me the clothes.

"Sure, no problem, that's cool . . ."

Calm on the outside, losing my shit on the inside.

" 'Cool'? Isn't that sweet? That was Braddy's favorite word. He had a wonderful vocabulary, but every other word out of his mouth was 'cool.' I'm just gonna go freshen up while you change. Would you like some cookies and milk?" she asks, like Oedipus' mother in pearls.

"Cookies and milk? Cool." I'm laying it on thick, but trying not to milk the cookies too hard.

She giggles like a crazy forty-year-old schoolgirl and leaves me alone in her dead son's room.

A Civil War rages in my head. The North says put on the outfit, then get the money. The South says get the money, then put on the outfit. After several bloody skirmishes the South relents, and I put on the outfit. But if she doesn't come back in with my money, that's it, I don't give a damn, I am going going gone.

The clothes fit like they were made for me. I look in the mirror. I look at Braddy in the khakis and Hawaiian shirt. Then I look back in the mirror.

I've disappeared.

Sure enough, as soon as my dad and I get to George Wallace Stadium, the heavens split and spit forth a furious wet rage, raindrops the size of manhole covers, hailstones the size of bowling balls, Zeus and Thor putting on a celestial heavymetal thunderlightshow that rocks the house.

So we turn right around and head back home, rain thrashing the roof, windshield, and hood as a black funnel gyroscopes toward us up George Wallace Drive.

I'm terribly impressed by all this weather. I'm not scared. My dad's driving, and he knows exactly what he's doing.

The sleet sheets down so heavy now we can't see two feet in front of us, and the twister whirls dervishly straight at us.

But my dad never stops. All the other drivers pull their cars over to the side of the road, but not my old man. He doesn't say anything and neither do I, but I'm awed by the squall as we crawl home through the tempest.

The next day, in the calm after the storm, when I look across the street at the house that sits up high on the hill, I see the twister has torn the roof clean off.

And my dad drove me through all of it, so I could play in a game that didn't even happen.

A flimsy blue negligee trimmed with black fox fur and red high heels walks through the door carrying a plate of brown cookies and a white glass of milk. Slimmy hips, pale belly, good gams nicely turned. Normally a sight like this would make my mojo corkscrew, but here, now, my heart plummets like the cable snapped, and I plunge fast, knowing there's a nasty crash coming and there's absolutely nothing I can do about it. Fevered hotsweats flash all over me, but I'm trying to keep this blank smile on my face, all the while wanting to scream, "Are you mad, woman? Go put some clothes on and check yourself into a clinic, where you can get some state-of-the-art mental-health care!"

But I don't.

"My husband gave me this and I never got a chance to wear it. Do you like it?"

My mommy trick strikes what's supposed to be a tarty pose, but she's so out of touch with her inner tart she ends up looking more like a mental patient than a sex baby.

"Have a cookie . . ."

She moves the plate of cookies toward me, and there it sits, half hidden under a cookie like an invitation to the gold miners' ball: my envelope.

Casually, oh-so-casually, I pick up the cookie over my envelope, take a bite out of it, then palm the sweet succor of my money into the back pocket of the dead Braddy's khakis. I'm a hundred bucks richer and I don't give a whatever about nothing. And the cookie's good. Moist. I like a moist cookie. I wash it down with the milk.

> *I'm done with the cookie,*
> *I'm ready for the nookie.*

I silently laugh at the poem in my head as I watch myself dressed in a Hawaiian shirt pretending to be the dead boy in the picture with his sexy mommy.

Envelope in hot pocket, cookie in cool belly, and devil-may-care upon my lips, I squint my eyes, and make her into the hottyhot porno star baby of my loverstudguy movie.

"Why don't you come over and sit on the bed with Mommy, Braddy? You don't mind if I call you Braddy, do you?" She smiles like Mother Mary on acid from the bed covered by the blanket with the sports guys on it.

"No, that's cool," I say.

Call me Braddy.

One Saturday afternoon when I'm ten I come home from playing ball, and the house is empty. This is unusual. My mother's home. I don't know how I know this, but I know it all the same. I call her name. She doesn't answer. I have a panic. Has she gotten sick of us, sick of Hueytown, sick of America, sick of her punishing husband? Worst of all, sick of me?

I check the house, my little heart pounding. She's gone. I know it. It never dawned on me that Mother might decide to bolt.

Breathing harder, I flopsweat into my parents' bedroom. She's not there. I go into the closet, where all the big pants and huge dresses live. The closet potpourri envelopes me: mothballs, shoe polish, and fresh laundry dancing together.

When I found her in there one time crying, it had seemed so odd and horrible. But now I'm actually hoping she's in there crying.

She's not.

I quicksand further into fear, and the more I squirm with the thought that she's gone, the faster I sink.

My pearly trick pats the bed next to her, the cue for Braddy to sit on the dead bed with his Crazy Mommy. Is it too late to give back the envelope and get the hell out? Yes, I believe it is. Just do what she wants and everything'll be fine, you'll get some ice cream, have a hang in 3-D, and see if Sunny's got some sweet young baby for you to swing with.

When I sit on the bed, Mommy pulls me into her and starts rocking. I'm confused. Does she want me to get sexy with her? Does she want me to be her little boy? I can barely breathe, suffocated by all this Mommy, her sickly-sweet perfume pounding on my temples.

She lies back on Braddy's bed and takes me with her. I end up embryonic, head on her chest. Then she guides my mouth to her breast, and dear dead Braddy is supposed to do the thing he's genetically designed for: suckle Mommy.

I take a breath. See myself spinning this yarn out for Sunny, and him whooping and *Et toi*ing. Hey, it's just another job, just another old broad for the chicken to bang.

So I suck.

Then she guides me on top of her, between her legs, and her hips stiltingly do a spasmodic grind while she fumbles with my zipper.

I fish myself out. Fish being the operative word. As in cold and limp. We have a problem, Houston. My eyes are clamped, because I don't want to see what's underneath me. So I position myself where I can get maximum rubbage, and with my eyes closed, I find the loverstudguy voice in my head:

"Oh, baby . . . give it to me you nasty little baby . . . you love it, don't you, baby? Oh, baby, baby, baby."

That gets the blood moving in the right direction. Next thing I know I'm inside her, swimming in that river again, and the water, as always, is good. Once you're in the river, it doesn't really matter how you got there, cuz the waterfall's always right up ahead.

"Do you love Mommy, Braddy?"

She grabs my head and puts me right in her face.

God I wish she hadn't said that. It jolts me right out of my river, and lands me smack-dab in the middle of this dead boy inside his mommy, who's got wet eyes I didn't even notice were crying, as she downloads her pain right into me.

I need to scream. I don't. I can't.

"Do you love Mommy, Braddy?"

She asks again, her voice cracking like a pane of dropped glass, wild eyes pleading with her dead son while she has sex with a boy whore.

Braddy's supposed to tell Mommy he loves her, but I can't get the words out of my mouth.

Until the need to please takes over.

"I love you, Mommy" somehow burbles out between my frozen lips.

She grabs my hips and starts pulling me into her hard, so I shut my eyes, and in the dark I manage to swim the good swim, slam the good slam, fight the good fight.

She pushes on my chest, which I suppose is a good thing, cuz she's also making little sex sounds.

Then she lurches, and I open my eyes just in time to see her lean her head over the side of the bed and unload a stream of sick onto the floor, the wave of vomit smell breaking all over me.

She pushes me off her like a mom lifting an automobile off her child who's trapped under the front tire. Then she bolts out of bed, and out the door.

I sit on the dead Braddy's bed, Mommy's secretions shining on me, and the smell of her sick cutting through me.

Frantic as only a ten-year-old boy can be, I bounce out the closet, down the hall, and through the back door. A huge acutely sloping backyard is behind the Alabama house. It could've been a ski jump if it ever snowed in Hueytown. Which of course it never did.

I glide the sliding-glass door open and run into the backyard. It's hot outside. You never realize in Alabama how cool the air-conditioning is inside until you step out into the inferno. Just walking out of the house I sweat, my blood pounding. I stand stock-still. Listen. I hear her. Crying. I can't see her yet, but I can hear her, and I'm comforted by the company of her misery.

My mother's leaning on a mammoth pine, sobbing in wet spasms. Next thing I know I'm holding her hand, and she's looking down at me, eyes deep swimming holes of sadness. I reach up hug high, and she wraps me in her arms, transfusing me with all that primal pain and absent love.

Gradually the swelling of my mom's sobs subsides, the tide rolls back out, and we walk hand in hand into the house, talking about thisandthat, nothing really, just easy talk.

My mom and I make cookies, the measuring, the beating, and the sifting pure succor, the smell of chocolate vanilla and butter melting me as it gets stronger and deeper, the treat of licking mixer blades, the raw dough slices of paradise, waiting, waiting, waiting, for the first warm bite to explode in my mouth, the ache buried once again beneath the silence.

Are we done? I don't know. I get out of bed, careful not to step in the sick on the floor. I take the envelope out of the pocket of Braddy's dead pants. I touch the hundred-dollar bill. That's better. Normally I want my tip, and God knows I earned it, but today I feel like a diver surfacing too fast, my insides bending, and if I don't get out of here quick, my brain's gonna explode.

I ditch Braddy's clothes, whip into my nuthugging elephant-bells and my too-tight Jimi Hendrix T, slip into my red high-tops, and deposit my cash in my pocket. Normally pocketing my sexmoney is the highlight of any job. Not today.

I shoot like infected sperm out of Braddy's room. But I can't leave yet. I have to make sure she's okay. I tiptoe down the hall and peek in the bedroom. It's long-day's-journey-into-night dark in there. I hear a little mumbly snuffly sound.

"Uh . . . excuse me . . ." I say softly.

More mumbles and snuffles.

"Um . . . I was just wondering if you're . . . okay." Louder this time, poking my head further into the room.

Mumbles. Snuffles.

"Do you need . . . are you all right?" I say so I know she'll hear me.

Her head snaps up like a hungry turtle surprised in the middle of lunch.

"Do you want more money? Is that what you want? There's more money on the desk in the den, take whatever you want, but please, just go . . ." Her face is all puffy red mad like Lady Macbeth at the end when she's trying to get that damn spot out.

It's like looking at a wounded animal bleeding in the middle of the road. You have to stop the car and get out and help. Don't you?

"Are you sure you don't want—"

"Just go! *GO!*"

Her shriek curdles my blood, and bolts me down the hall. But even now, I need my money. That's how empty I am. So I jam into the den and open a fancy-looking box on the desk, where a wad of cash stares at me. Gotta be five hundred bucks there. My first impulse is to clean her out. Hey, I earned it. But I can't. I take fifty, put the rest back, and with my C and a half I steamroll down the hall, through the kitchen, and out the back door.

Oh God.

12. Peas & Cornbread

Going down, sir!

—DROOPY DOG

I finger my pager. It's become my antitalisman bad-luck charm. I'm having a lot of trouble rolling that big huge rock up that big huge mountain this morning, sitting in Existentialism, trying to focus on Sister Tiffany and the meaning of life. Her mouth is moving but, unfortunately, I can't hear a word she's saying. Usually I spend quality Existentialism time staring at Kristy, dreaming about the sweet little life we're gonna have together.

Not today.

"Do you love Mommy, Braddy?"

That voice keeps ringing in the bell tower of my head. I see myself in the Hawaiian shirt and khakis looking at myself in the mirror next to the picture of Braddy in the Hawaiian shirt and khakis. Dad blowing his brains out with a shotgun, Braddy all boozed up driving head-on into a bus, Mommy washing that shirt over and over until all her dead son's blood is gone.

"Do you love Mommy, Braddy?"

I thought about trying to call Kristy after I left the Palisades. I actually had the phone in my hand, but I couldn't pull the trigger. I felt mean. Wanted to pick a fight. So I went out and bought my day-old birthday cake and my tub of ice cream, and I ate it all up. But still I felt hungry enough to have sex with a horse. I tried to sleep, but that was a complete joke.

So I went to Sunny's. Three-D was business as usual. The Dixie Chickens fighting and French-kissing. Cruella and Sunny doing the Temptations. People I never saw before and would never see again. Jade was not in attendance. I was sad about that. Sunny hugged me, kissed me on both cheeks N'Awlins style, and tried to cop a feel.

"Hoo-ie, boy, if you ain't a sight for sore eyes. How's the job tonight, baby? Uh-oh, one of them, huh? Well, lemme getcha some Jack and a Jill."

He got me a shot of Jack Daniel's and then introduced me to a sweety-looking girl he'd christened Buttercup. When she wandered into the restaurant that afternoon, Sunny'd sprinkled some magic fairy dust on her, and *poof!* Here she was in 3-D, hanging out with a smoking bong, giggling with a gaggle of freaks. She could be thirteen, could be fifteen, but she's certainly no more than sixteen. She's medium-size blondish corn-fed gaptooth bangs and ponytail cute. She couldn't really keep up with the lightning-fast 3-D banter, but the girl now called Buttercup was totally adorable in her little Daisy Duke cutoffs, duffel bag, and ruffly dorky mall shirt.

Sunny whispered that he wants me to break her in. She's my perk for doing a bang-up job. So after hanging awhile I took her back to my hovel. Ironic, I'm a one-boy sex factory, but I've never had a woman in my carpetwalled hellhole. Then again, I don't wanna shit where I live.

Buttercup is the essence of sweet, but there's definitely a FOR RENT sign in her eyes. Someone has clearly stuck a monkey wrench in Buttercup's gears. I wasn't sure whether she'd ever had sex, but Sunny put me in charge of making a chicken out of her, and I was taking my responsibility seriously.

I don't allow myself to consider that I might be doing a disservice to Buttercup by being her sexwork facilitator. I couldn't. I was sure I was doing her a favor transforming her from a no-skills runaway to a breadwinning chicken, getting her off the streets, where she was sure to get the shit repeatedly kicked out of her.

I laid out the whole thing, soup to nuts, for the girl now called Buttercup. Guess what the first lesson was?

GET THE MONEY UP FRONT

After I briefed her on the ins and outs of independent sex contracting, we moved to the hands-on section of the tutorial. She was an enthusiastic student, and her learning curve steep, especially in her oral exam, which she passed with flying colors. More important, she had that eager-to-please, turned-off turned-on quality that's crucial in the making of a first-class whore. Plus, of course, she was dead broke, hungry, had no resources, no home, no family to take care of her, and nowhere in the whole world to go, which helps.

Then I was swimming in the river with the girl now called Buttercup, endorphin dolphins frolicking beside me, and when the spray of the waterfall hit my face, everything seemed right with the world.

But here, now, the day after, in Existentialism class, I can't stop fingering my pager.

"Does Braddy love Mommy?"

The top of my head feels like it's about to pop off.

Finally, mercifully, class is over, and I bolt fast. I hope Kristy's following me. I need Kristy to follow me. I decide if Kristy's following me, the gods are on my side. As I walk down the hill overlooking Hollywood onto the immaculate lawn, the air rejuvenates and the sun revives me. It's a clean day, cuz it's windy, and you can see all the way to the ocean. I deepbreathe, smell the warm grass, and wait for Kristy, trying to look like a normal Joe College guy enjoying his existential sun-drenched afternoon, instead of a chicken on his day off waiting for a girl like his life depends upon it.

But there's no Kristy.

I'm used to craving the normal of her, but today the craving's consuming me. I realize now I need to take her out to lunch, talk about nuns, drink a few beers, maybe even have some old-fashioned American apple-pie sex. I wait and wait, barely able to contain myself, ants multiplying in my pants every second.

Finally, when I've stood all I can stand, I go hunting for Kristy. Back in class Sister Tiffany gabs with a few stragglers. I chainsaw down to the library. Nothing. Back to the lawn. Nothing. As I walk into the cafeteria, I bump into someone. My fist has a life of its own, and it clenches without authorization from upper management. Luckily I stop it before it can rise up in anger. Then my polite British schoolboy takes over, and I'm an apologizing machine, saying sorry so often the apologizee looks at me like I escaped from Bedlam. I turn off the sorry button and scan the lunchroom. No Kristy, no Kristy, no Kristy. Jam back up the hill. Check the lawn. No Kristy. Some serious snark is clogging my pipes. I want to smash a mirror with a five-iron, crack a skull with a brick, smash my hand through a TV screen. If I don't find this girl I can't stand to be around for more than a night at a clip, I am seriously gonna do something very bad.

My mom and dad buy a Winnebago trailer when I'm ten, hitch it to the back of the faux-wood-paneled station wagon, and off we go to look for America.

The Grand Canyon invites us into Mother Earth. Old Faithful is a holy explosion from the blowhole of the planet, one you can set your watch by. We redwood forest and Gulf Stream water. Glacial ice creeps down a mountain slower than time. We gather driftwood like old sailors' bones and make a bonfire where spirits of Chippewa shaman dance. We see bears, meeses, and now and then a beaver.

My mom and dad embrace America more fully than any born-and-bred Americans I've ever seen. They show us the nooks and crannies of warm sweet lakes, a Petrified Forest, and the Great White Way.

And I never thanked them for that.

Kristy.

She's standing in a shaft of golden California sunlight, looking like Madonna, Mother of Jesus Christ our Lord and Savior, writing a note by my motorcycle.

Kristy, Kristy, Kristy!!!

I'm way too happy to see this girl.

I sneak up behind her and wrap my fingers around her eyes. After a flinch reflex she realizes it's me, and when she relaxes back into my arms, everything in Chickenville suddenly seems A-Okay on this sunny day.

"Sister Tiffany?" says Kristy.

"You didn't tell anybody about us, did you?" I ask.

"Hell, no," she says.

"You swear to God?" I ask.

"I swear to God, Sister—"

I spin Kristy around, and she's all shocked surprise—

"I mean, David, um . . . how's it hangin'?"

"So, you and Sister Tiffany?" I smile.

"You don't mind?" She bats eyelashes.

I always forget how funny Kristy is.

"No, I always wanted to have a three-way with a nun," I say. "Wanna go for a ride?"

"Where?"

"Your place."

I kiss her lips, which are once again not too thin at all.

"Are you serious?" she asks.

"Sure."

This is turning out so much better than I imagined.

"Well, I was supposed to go to the library, but . . . okay, sure, why not . . ." she says, very Holly Golightly.

But again the gods toy with me, for just as I've finally forgotten all about it, my pager goes off.

At the dinner table when I'm eight, my immigrant father slurpsucks translucent fat globules off pickled pig's feet as my brother and sisters and I take turns telling what great American things we did that day.

My six-year-old runty logicdriven towheaded mathgenius brother loathes peas with a searing passion, and tonight he's decided he will eat no more of them. My mom speaks to him about his peas. He ignores her. Finally, when she presses, he announces in a grown-up voice, "I'm not going to eat any more peas."

My mother makes a show of consternation, but you can tell her heart's not in it, and the whole thing's going to blow over in a moment.

Except a burr's in the bug up my dad's ass.

"Eat yer bluddy peas," spits my father.

This is odd. He never interferes with the raising of his children. So I assume my little brother will just cave and eat his peas.

To my shock and amazement, he stares my dad down.

This is getting fun.

My pager going off sends shots of sex and fear and dread and money slamming into my solar plexus, and I snap shut without even being aware I'm snapping shut.

And I do it right in front of Kristy.

"Is everything all right?" She drags me back from my torture chamber.

"No, I'm fine. Sure, yeah . . . I'm fine, everything's fine."

But the more I say how fine everything is, the less fine it seems.

"Is there anything I can do?" Kristy's all genuine concern.

"No, it's a work thing. I gotta make a call . . ." I give her a thin gruel of a smile, trying to stay loose when I feel tighter than a bodybuilder's ass.

"You want me to come with you?" Kristy's full of care.

"No!" I say, too loud and harsh, and I want the word back even before it even leaves my mouth.

Can we do a second take on that?

Kristy sighs. Suddenly I've gone from sweet boyfriend to harsh freak.

"David, what is it? What's the matter?" Kristy stands there and asks.

And I love her for that.

The scary silence is back at the dining-room table, like in one of those westerns when some feller accuses some other feller of cheatin' and everybody's waitin' fer the first gun to be drawn.

"Eat those bluddy peas or I'll stot summink off yer bluddy heed," my father barks.

"Stot" is bounce. "Heed" is head. Clearly he means business. But my runty brother will not be moved.

"You will sit in that bluddy chair till you finish those bluddy peas." My father's head reddens and his veins bulge as I picture myself loosening a valve on the back of his head and watching the steam blow out his ears like an old-fashioned cartoon work whistle.

In slow motion my brother forks one pea, painfully places it in his mouth, and with strained face forces the poison pellet down his gullet.

Silence. More silence. Crazy straining silence.

After three more excruciating peas go down, everyone

resumes their happy banter. Except my dad. He says nothing. I'm laughing my ass off inside. My little genius brother's twisting our father on his own rack.

"Hey, I'm sorry, I really am. My boss, he's . . . got it in for me, he's been riding my ass. But I'm really sorry . . ."

I backpedal and shadowbox for all I'm worth.

"I'm confused. What do you . . . do exactly?"

"Deliveries . . . packages, envelopes, scripts, you know. I go to Malibu, or Beverly Hills, or the Valley, and if I work at night, or do emergency jobs, it's really good money. And since my parents cut me off, I gotta make money. It's a great job, except for my asshole boss . . ." I lean in confidentially. "He wants to, you know . . . seduce me."

"Oh my God, that's illegal. Do you want me to tell my dad, cuz he could maybe—"

Obviously I don't want Daddy in my beeswax.

"No, that's okay, I talked to the owner. He's on my side. And I don't wanna lose my job."

"Sure, absolutely. Well, I'm sorry. If there's anything I can do, just ask, okay?"

Just ask. The way she says it, it seems like the easiest thing in the world.

"Lemme go make this call, and . . . I'll be right back . . ." I move in now, all denial and survival. "And I'm really sorry. Will you forgive me?"

"Of course," says Kristy. "I'm just glad you felt you could trust me enough to tell me the truth."

"Yeah . . ." I nod.

I almost believe it all myself.

My dad takes out his fury on the innocent plates and dishes, and even as I'm putting the last bit of roast beef in my mouth, he's snatching, jerking, and cleaning my plate. He flings knives and forks into the dishwater *zing zing zing*, wrestles with the pots and pans, cleansing and purging them faster than humanly possible, slamming them back into the cupboards *twang bang clang*. Then he roars off to the couch, rams on the big TV, and snores in a feverish rhythm.

Years later I'll read the Edgar Allan Poe story about a guy who kills some old codger, buries him under the house, then goes insane when he hears the dead man's heart pounding louder and louder, until he can't stand it anymore and confesses to the cops.

That's how I remember my father's snores.

Mr. Hartley has a job for me, a good job, right now, two hundred dollars.

"Absolutely, Mr. Hartley. I'm all over it."

Mr. Hartley chuckles.

"Excellent. David, we've had great feedback, and your client from Saturday was very complimentary."

"I appreciate that, it means a lot to me . . . Thanks."

I'm genuine. I'm real. This is so rare for me right now. And I'm able to do it with my pimp easier than the girl I'm falling in love with.

"So I was curious what happened on Monday . . ."

I can hear the sinister pipe organ creeping in the background as Mr. Hartley switches gears all over me. My breath is gone. What did I do? What did I not do? What did she say? What kind of shit am I in now? Does Braddy love Mommy?

"Uh . . . nothing. Why . . . did she say something?"

A vise squeezes my temples as I tremble.

"Why don't you tell me exactly what happened?" Mr. Hartley's a cagey bastard.

Say as little as possible, and when in doubt say even less.

"Well . . . it was just a normal job, you know . . ."

I don't think I can say anything less than that.

"Did she seem . . . upset?"

If I say she wasn't upset, he'll know I'm a liar, but if I say she was upset, then am I responsible for whatever bad shit came down in the wake of my home visit?

"Uh . . . yeah. I guess she was a little upset. But I didn't do anything, I swear to God . . ." I'm tap-dancing as fast as I can, and Mr. Hartley feels me all the way from Immaculate Heart College to Sunset Boulevard.

"I'm not accusing you of anything. I just want you to tell me exactly what happened." Mr. Hartley's now using his no-more-messing-around voice.

I suppress a sigh of great weight.

"Well, yeah, she did seem upset. But it wasn't my fault, I swear to God. She even gave me a tip . . ." I'm covering my ass, so there's not one pink little inch of it showing.

"David"—Mr. Hartley does that thing grown-ups do when they start a sentence with your name—"we're not accusing you of anything. That's why I gave you this job today, to let you know we're very pleased with your work. But I need to know what happened. Now think carefully."

"Well, to tell you the truth, she seemed kinda . . ."

I don't want to say the word, but I have a feeling he's gonna make me.

"She seemed kinda what?" asks Mr. Hartley.

"Well, kinda . . . crazy."

There. I said it.

Pause. Long pause.

"I don't want you talking to anybody about this. Nobody. Do you understand?" Mr. Hartley's dead-serious scares the shit outta me.

"Yes, absolutely. No, I mean, I never talk to anybody, about anything." I'm playing jump rope with my own tongue.

"The client had a . . . problem." Mr. Hartley's voice flatlines.

"What happened?" Sweat drips down my rib cage.

"The less you know the better."

The way Mr. Hartley says it, I know this part of the conversation is over, which is just fine with me, cuz I never want to think about this shit for the rest of my life.

So I swallow it all whole, and lock it in my pressure cooker, where it will feed on me until I can get rid of it.

"I might have something for you this weekend. I'm just waiting for a confirmation." Mr. Hartley's back to being buttah.

"Excellent. I'll make sure the pager's on vibrate."

Mr. Hartley's wry chuckle is highly gratifying.

He disconnects from me while I disconnect from myself. Did Mommy slit her wrist in a bubblebath? Swallow a bottle of pills? Suck on an antique pistol? She seemed like the dramatic type.

Change the record, Braddy.

My little brother sits at the dinner table till eleven o'clock that night, when he forces down his last poison pea. We're all supposed to be asleep of course, but it's much too exciting for that.

He looks so small as he opens our bedroom door, back-lighted like a hero, one small boy standing tall against the Man. He smiles a funny little smile. I want to tell him how great he is, but already the silence has its hand around my throat.

"What time is it?"

I already know it's eleven.

"Eleven," he says.

"Did you get grounded?" I say.

"Not yet," says he.

He gets into bed. We lie there, not sleeping, coconspirators in a rich secret rebellion. We don't have peas again for a long time.

I go back to Kristy, tell her I gotta work, kiss her good-bye, then go to a prestigious Beverly Hills hotel for my two-hundred-dollar job. She's a big-boned sweet-faced executive from some Midwestern beefy beer-soaked wonderbread place, who's in town for business and heard from a girlfriend who's friends with Frannie about the service. About me. God love Frannie.

Midwest wants to talk. Wants someone to be nice to her. I talk. I'm nice. Easy Money. She has the surf-and-turf special. She's nice and she's nervous, but when she finally calms down, she really gets into it. I'm working on the whole woman's pleasure-garden-of-earthly-delight thing, and Midwest digs it.

I do have a flash of slime as I wash up afterward and get caught in the mirror staring at the miserable plucked chicken who stares back at me. But I have a whole system now. I feel the warm cookie of my money, and focus on 3-D and all the treats waiting for me after my trick. This gets me up, out, and over to Sunny's, where I eat ribs slaw and jalapeño cornbread, and suck on beer booze and bong. In 3-D you can be liked, admired, and respected even if you are a houseboy. We have our own chicken language, customs, and jokes, just like lawyers, Freemasons, and astronauts, and I love being part of that. I dip the cornbread into the barbecue sauce and it lights up the inside of my mouth. I'm hungry all the time these days. Lots of day-old birthday cake and tubs of ice cream. But tonight, in 3-D, mercifully, I manage somehow to get full.

When Sunny touches me on the shoulder like family, he makes me feel like I'm King Shit living the High Life.

"Boy, Ah gotta big-time opportunity for your ass. An' Ah do mean your ass. Friday night, big ol' costume party, an' you is coe-jully invited. Welcome to the Show, bay-bay!" Sunny does a whoopholler and a funny little dance.

"What do you mean?" I'm equal dollops excitement and terror.

"It's a costume bawl, an' there's gonna be boocoo bucks there, boy. Mo' money, mo' money, mo' money . . ." Sunny's a hog in heaven, lowering his voice as he moves in for the kill. "An' Mamma needs a new pair of shoes."

This is why Sunny is master pimp. He ties all his love into my ability to make him money.

13. Tinkerbell & a Baby Bulldog

You're nobody till somebody loves you.

—DEAN MARTIN

Blue nuthugging elephantbells tight as the traffic will allow, sleeveless white T, red high-tops, and black wraparound Ray•Bans. This is the state-of-the-art, goin'-to-the-orgy ensemble Sunny's chosen for me, and when he finishes primping, preening, and mother-henning me, he closes his eyes to cleanse his visual palette, then pops them open and gives me the once-over twice. Then he grins.

"Yeaaaaaaah, bay-bay."

And suddenly it's all good.

As Moby Dick glides gracefully through the gilded gargoyle gates of the gaudy Mulholland mansion, limos lounge languidly, Alfa Romeos pose pompously, and Jaguars graze gluttonously on the punch-drunk pavement.

Butterflies flutter by in my belly. I feel like Cinderella with my glass sneakers, Moby Dick pumpkin, and pimp Fairy Godmother.

Our all-American rocketship crash-lands again when I'm eight, this time in Virginia, Minnesota, where one-hundred-and-seven-year-old Scandihoovian men in the forty-seven-below dead of winter jump nude through a hole they cut in the ice, plunge into freezing-cold lake water, then sprint back to the one-hundred-and-seven-degree sauna. When you go outside, your breath forms little icicles on your eyebrows, eyelashes, and 'stache, if you have one. Ten thousand lakes, complete with one billion summer skeeters big as World War II bombers that suck your blood like black bug vampires.

My dad's explosives corporation has sent him to the Mesabi Range that runs just south of the Canadian border so he could strip-mine the mountain. So they're cutting down the trees, blowing holes in the virgin earth, and scooping out its guts.

One winter the snow's so high we climb up on the roof and jump off, flying through the sky, landing in a snowcloud, and sinking slow, swallowed by all that soft cold whiteness, like diving into an ice-cream cone.

The mansion's supported by huge white marble phalli swimmimg in seas of roses sleeping peacefully in their beds. The door must be twenty feet high, with a giant lionheaded doorknocker that looks like it would love to take a bite out of your hand.

Sunny gives me the wink and the smile.

I can do this. Woman's pleasure. Loverstudguy.

When Sunny gives the lionheaded knocker a knock, a seven-foot doorman dressed as a dormouse opens the door as regally as a giant dressed like a rodent can.

Huge music pulsates through the booming woofer-happy sound system. Overhead a chandelier twinkles like a big drag queen on Halloween. Underfoot the marble floor lies cold, majestic, and butch.

Sunny's a puffed-up rutting peacock who tows me like a houseboatboy into the mansion.

"Hooooooo-ie, Sunny is in de house!"

Voices retort by the score: "Sunny!!!" "Look what the cat dragged in!" "And the cat has brought a chicken!"

Sunny's got a line for everyone. A slick wink, a knowing nod, a sticky innuendo. Hundreds of eyeballs train their periscopes on me, and I'm awash in the warm wet heat.

It's one of those times in my life when you know things are either gonna get a lot better or a lot worse.

Marlene Dietrich cruises by with Attila the Hun. Dr. Strangelove's pushed in his wheelchair by Mae West. A six-foot-two Amazon Snow White in a leopard bikini is surrounded by three dwarfs dressed as Doc, Grumpy, and the sleaziest Sneezy I've ever seen. A behemoth clad in a black leather Death mask, studded collar with leash attached, and rhinestone codpiece walks by on all fours, ridden by a tiny Japanese Madame Butterfly Lady Godiva woman in heavy Kabuki makeup, lashing him lovingly with her cat-o'-nine-tails.

I feel right at home.

The Minnesota snow is high when I'm eleven. My father's gone, blowing up the mountain.

My mother and I try to midwife our bulldog Gwenyvere, who bulges heavy with puppies, belly distended to monstrous proportions, panting on old blankets.

My mom strokes Gwenyvere's head, talking soft and sweet to her while I pet her rump, wet helpless bulldog confusion swelling in Gwenyvere's red-blood eyes. She's begging me to help her. I want to help her. I just don't know how.

Then Gwenyvere goes into hard labor, straining painfully panting and pushing, thick muscles taut tight.

But the pups will not come.

The pups will not come.

The pups will not come.

There are three populations at the Big Ball.

The Olde Bastards: puffy, gray, and rich.

The Middle Men: Fagins making quick, slick bucks.

The Freaks, Chickens, and Chickadees: leering leather and young flesh, bruised bodybuilders and cheerleaders, cool schoolgirls and hot haunted jocks.

The Olde Bastards clearly have a personal relationship with Death, who sits in their living room waiting. We're their Fountain of Youth, and they want to drain us dry.

I watch myself watching them watching us, wrapped in the womb of my scar tissue.

Sunny leads me into the reddest room I've ever seen, where a long wooden table leans against the wall like a Noah's Ark of liquor, and two bartenders wearing nothing but hockey masks, cock rings, and black leather gloves wordlessly serve.

A cornucopia of mind-bending brain-numbers are laid out attractively in antique crystal mint dishes: buttons of peyote, magic mushrooms and mda/x, Maui Zaui Hurricane Swirl, Afghani Moses Bull Rush, and Moroccan Fez Blower.

Sunny gives me a silver spoonful of mda/x, and a jolt explodes in my head, as if someone has gently inserted a lit firecracker into my cranium. Then a warm tingly itsy-bitsy spider creeps up my waterspout. I want to soak in a giant vat of spumoni, and swim in the river and feel the waterfall spray in my face.

Into the long thick night, my mother and I try to pull puppies out of poor dear Gwenyvere, as she shudders shoving moaning groaning growling howling desperate to deliver.

But the pups will not come.

My mom frantically leaves the vet emergency messages, while Gwenyvere collapses whimpering, head bowed, breath gone.

I lie down with her, nose to smashed-in nose, and when she looks into my eyes I see resignation has moved in. Gwenyvere's eyes shut now with a huge heaving sigh, like her heart lung machine was just unplugged.

For the first time I think she will die.

Peter Pan's wearing green stiletto hump-me pumps, green silk stockings and garter, green satin opera-length gloves, plunging green velvet strapless gown, slit to the hilt, and she's packed in puffy tight, flesh hanging out here there and everywhere.

In one hand she grips a whip with a phallic handle, in the other a leash attached to a small young woman in a white wig wearing nothing but a sparkling light on her head.

Tinkerbell.

Sunny jumps in, all Southern smooth, and dishes out the introductions.

"This here is Peter Pan, and . . . Tinkerbell . . ."

"Hello." She's stiff as flint.

"Hi." Tinkerbell smiles shy with high-beam eyes. "I'm from Never-Never Land."

"Hi," says I, "I'll never grow up."

Tinkerbell is so naked.

Ms. Pan whispers into Sunny, and he leans back laughing.

"Boy, why dohncha dance with Tinkerbell?" Sunny gives me the nod.

With the mda/x, the buzz from the desperate wanting of the Olde Bastards, the adrenaline racehorsing through me, and the soundtrack pounding, I'm mad to go Tinkerbelling.

Peter Pan unhooks her leash, and the girl wearing nothing but the light over her white wig sways with the music. She's small all over. Little-girl hands and feet. Little freckles. And, like all my poultry peers, sometimes she's twelve, sometimes she's forty.

Then she looks at me with big crooning baby blues, and we're rhythmically in sync, in utero, bump for bump, grind for grind, tribal shaking, lust loose in a loin lock, lost in each other's music.

Tinkerbell digs herself into my shoulders. I yowl and thump her into me so our chests hit hard. My teeth rip into her neck with nothing but sheer instinct, and Tinkerbell screams in blood pleasure.

I suck hard on a mouthful of her neck. Pulling my hair hard, she rips my head from her flesh, where a red welt blossoms. I growl and smack a loud slap on her ass. Tinkerbell's on fire with desire, high and higher, and lashes her tongue out yelping, piercing her nails into my back. I shout cuz it feels good while it hurts, heavy lovesweat flying off us as the crowd oozes and ahs, and all that juice fills me and thrills me—damn this is the most fun I have ever had in my life.

Me and Tink could move to the Smoky Mountains, build a cabin in the woods, raise cornonthecob, and have little freak babies.

I can see it so clearly.

Suddenly, in the thick hard dark of the cold black night, a huge white baby bulldog head appears from between Gwenyvere's hind legs. Eyes closed, it hangs half in the world and half in the womb. Then shoulders ribs hindquarters and feet plop out with great gobs of goo, and a perfect baby dog slides onto the blanket in a puddle of blood and guts and Godknowswhat.

Lord, it's a big ol' pup. Enormous. Doesn't seem anatomically possible that this huge thing could come out of her, and I just watched it happen.

Gwenyvere, the proud new mother, is relieved beyond belief, and pops out two much smaller pups, half as big, easy as you please, then happily starts slurping off the thin clear sausage shrink-wrap covering them.

My mom and I dance like punch-drunk midwives as the pups squirm when she laps them with that huge wet tongue. Watching those new pups vibrating with life, there's no way around it: This is a miracle.

The strobe light turns everything into stop-action kinetic Picasso orgy snapshots. Slender arms pendulum breasts thigh cheese lip meat calves dangling bloodbank eyes and shaved coochies stick together in impossible angles.

Tinkerbell's giving me more pleasure than seems humanly possible, vaporlocked on me, dancing the mouth mambo.

Osweetbabyjesusmothermaryandjoseph.

I look down at Tinkerbell, who looks up at me at the exact same instant, like we've rehearsed the move many times, and we smile dreamy creamy smiles at each other. I could rescue her from this Peter Pan asshole. We could start our own chicken business, Marx style, from each according to ability, to each according to need. We could make a shitload of money, then go live on an island somewhere. Make beautiful babies that get brown in the sun. I wish I knew her name.

The crowd crowds round, leaning in so they won't miss a trick, the heat of the spotlight even hotter as Peter Pan flicks Tinkerbell with her whip and Tink wraps herself around me. The crowd sucks a gasp. I close my eyes and the rapture flows through Tinkerbell and into me in an endless sensuous Möbius strip.

With careful orchestration, split-second timing, and shrewd momentum management, Sunny has turned me, the simple son of immigrants, into the catalyst for a take-no-prisoners, lifestyles-of-the-rich-and-famous, old-fashioned newfangled orgy.

That's why I love America.

Eyes shut tiny tight, the puppies wiggle and wriggle and squiggle on the blanket, getting the life licked into them by Gwenyvere, who's mama-bulldog proud.

My mother and I shake hands, shake our heads, and make

many happy sounds while those teeny-tiny puppies twist and fidget, trying to figure out what the hell's going on in this big old world.

Then I notice the first, too-huge baby. It's not moving. Gwenyvere won't touch the still giant. She pushes the other two away from it hard with her smushed-in face, then licks them like baby bulldog Popsicles.

My mom looks at me. Gwenyvere seems too busy loving the alive pups to care that her firstborn is lying lifeless in after-birth. My mother puts the huge not-moving one next to Gwenyvere, but she shoves it with her muzzle all the way off the blanket. Then she goes back to mothering her other pups.

Oh, my. That big baby bulldog is dead.

Tinkerbell showers me with snowflake kisses, a mad hunger flowing between us as we ride around on each other in the middle of this love zoo at the height of mating season.

Yeah, an island somewhere in the South Pacific. We'll rent a hut on the beach for fifty cents a day. Catch fish, eat mangoes, roll around in the sunset.

Then I hit a spot in Tinkerbell and she pours, soaring into me, roaring a Jungle scream.

The orgy comes to a full stop, and we're once again right in the center of America, all eyes upon us and oh, it's good in there, one big writhing amoeba feeding me, feeding her.

Peter Pan eyeballs me mean and hard. She grabs Tinkerbell and with a loud popping sound drags her away.

Tink looks back sadly at me. She doesn't want to go. I don't want her to go. Then she disappears through the Sea of Freaks back to Never-Never Land.

Deadweight of giant pup in hands, thick and dumbfounded in my parka as the hard day is born, it's my job to bury the huge lifeless baby bulldog.

It's cold as death this morning. I brush snow from the ground and put the still life down, his eyes locked shut forever.

I try to dig a grave, but the shovel bounces off the stone ground, and Mother Earth will not open herself and accept this little dead baby.

The deceased white pup's the same color as the snow.

Finally I manage to chisel the shallowest of graves, and into the dark hard hole I put the baby giant. I cover it up with dirt and snow, then look up and try to pray. But I have nothing to say, and it seems like no one is up there.

I'm in Hump Time Zone for I know not how long, in and out of more holes than a hungry gopher. A tattoo of a shark swims across a Botticelli bottom. A Ku Klux Klan Grand Wizard has his white bottom paddled by a man Aunt Jemima. The three-hundred-pound behemoth is forced into positions of humiliation by the ninety-pound Madame Butterfly, who whips him until welts sprout like fleshflowers, then whispers sweet nothings in his ear.

Suddenly I come to, like a caterpillar awakening from a butterfly dream. I look over at Sunny and he nods at me, opening a side door.

Then we're floating home in our Moby Dick pumpkin chariot through the alabaster night, a black crow hanging high in front of a big fat moon.

"Ya done good, boy," Sunny says.

"Thanks, Sunny," comes up out of me.

I finally feel good.

For about ten seconds. Then I want someone to suffer like I do.

14. Hoop Rage

Anger is a short madness.

—HORACE

Below Immaculate Heart College, halfway down the hill, lives the basketball court. There's not alotta sports action at IHC, it being a nun school and all, but this afternoon there's a nice three-on-three situation working as the sun continues its perpetual Hollywood shine. My fellow hoopsters are out for a little lite hoops, looking to break a mini-sweat, knock down some Js, go hard to the hole, do some minor white-boy smacking.

Me, I'm having one of those days. Layups roll around the rim before dribbling off miserably. Passes clang off my frying-pan hands. Jumpers thud hard off iron. I'm throwing up enough bricks to build a house with my three little piggie friends, and I can just see the Big Bad Wolf hiding behind a tree waiting to eat my grandmother.

I'm swearing loud now. I'm a very good swearer. It's a kind of speaking-in-tongues, ecstatic religious release for me.

"Cocksuckingpigbastardscumsuckingpissboy!"

Everyone's looking at me funny, like there might be something wrong with me. Whatever. There's nothing in my universe now but this silly little pickup game, and the rage bubbling up in deep wells, where I've stored it away for just this kind of occasion.

My dad is recruited when I'm thirteen by an explosives start-up in Useless, Texas, to be the executive in charge of getting shit done, so the next stop on our All-American Dream Tour is Dallas, thirty miles from Useless. Actually it's Euless, but everybody calls it Useless.

You'll know why if you ever go to Useless.

My mom doesn't see my dad for days at a time, and when he is around he eats, sleeps, and attacks the yard with power tools at the same furious pace.

But now he's an Executive. The milk and the honey are here at last. The coal miner's son is striking gold.

Bumping, grinding, and shoving on my guy, I'm digging the hitting, goading him to retaliate. And the madder I get the worser I play. The ball's bouncing off my knee, fumbling through my hands, and sliding through my butterfingers.

I'm D-ing up on my guy now. He tries to drive past me, only I slide over and hip-check him, flashing one of my Minnesota hockey moves in Tinsel Town. I knock him off balance, and he loses the ball out-of-bounds.

He calls a foul.

"Foul? Bullshit! That's no foul. You think that's a foul? That's just good D making you look bad, baby!"

My guy looks around sheeplike, seeking support from his

teammates, who shuffle around like they're looking for spare change, not wanting to get dragged into my theater of cruelty.

Finally a guy on my team sighs. "Yeah, man, I thought you fouled him."

And this guy's on *my* team.

"That's a foul? Oh, I'm sorry, I didn't realize we were playing pussyball. I wish someone had told me."

I grab the ball and put it right in my guy's face. "Okay," I say, "let's play some pussyball."

My guy looks at me like I'm a genetic engineering project gone horribly wrong.

I can barely focus on the game now, just waiting for the opportunity to pound the shit out of my guy, who's getting rid of the ball too quick, watching me out the corner of his eye, giving me too much room when I have the ball.

I bide my time, crouched low in the tall grass while the angrypsycho talks on the audio track in my brain: You wanna see a foul, I'll show you a foul, ya pieceoshitmotherbastardcum-burpingbitch.

Then suddenly my golden moment unfolds in slow motion as my guy turns the corner dribble-driving around the foul line. He's lost track of me, thinks he beat me to the spot, but I'm one step ahead of him, playing hide-and-seek behind his teammate.

And now he's mine.

As my guy leaves his feet to go up for the layup, he's slightly off balance, concentrating on the rim, while I line him up in the crosshairs, coiling, poised, spring-loaded with stored-up venom.

My body is all growed up when I'm fifteen. I play soccer with my dad's team in Dallas, and they're a very good team, league champs, mostly expatriate Brits. Playing against a brutish team, a burly stocky defender viciously hacks me. I crumble, howling, clutching my Achilles' heel where I've been violated. I get up tough, so all my dad's teammates know what a cold-blooded bastard I am, and tell the hard man who hit me to piss off. My old man busts over and, after he makes sure I'm okay, points at my attacker, and marks him with the evil eye.

About ten minutes later the marked man gets the ball, and out of nowhere my old man materializes and eviscerates him like a knight slaying the Jabberwocky. The other team goes mad, and the ref threatens to expel my dad from the game. But he stands tall over my fallen attacker and tosses me a little wink that no one else can see.

My dad has punished mine enemy.

I fly at my guy, high on bile, and slam the sharp blade of my shoulder into his sternum, OH MY GOD it feels good, that deep-down bodycrunch, me solid mass, him off-kilter bantamweight, the visceral inflicting thrill pulsing through my pleasure centers.

His body jackknifes backward, torso slingshotting away, while his bottom half stays where it is for a moment, then follows the top half, knees and elbows akimbo.

He hits the asphalt with his left elbow and the side of his left knee, scraping layers of skin onto the asphalt, and grinding to a halt with shocked pain spreading across his face.

"Is that a foul? Cuz where I come from, that's what we call a foul!" I roar, towering over him like a false god.

My guy touches the open wound on his knee, and his hand comes back with blood. He touches his elbow. More blood. He looks from the blood to me. Back to the blood. Then back to me.

"What the hell is wrong with you?" The hurt of a child who's been punished for no reason at all.

I could've broken his ribs. We could be scraping his brain off the blacktop. What the hell *is* wrong with me?

Everyone stares at me like I'm unfit for human company. I shrink instinctively and trot out the apologia.

"Sorry, man. I'm so sorry. I guess I'm a little . . ."

A little what? Psycho? Homicidal?

I reach out my hand to help him up. He turns it down.

"You got a problem, man."

Everyone agrees. They help him up.

"Hey, I'm sorry man, that's just the way we play where I come from." Where's that, Sing Sing? "Your ball, man, sorry." I'm trying to pretend everything's normal, but nobody's playing along.

"No, I'm done," my guy mumbles, hobbling away like a war hero after a senseless bombing.

Then I'm alone, the hole in my bucket a little bigger.

15. Here Cum de Judge

Power tends to corrupt, and absolute power corrupts absolutely.

—LORD ACTON

"We're having a big bash at my parents' house on Easter, and I was wondering if you wanted to come."

And there it is. Kristy has invited me to her mommy and daddy's house, with Suicidal Sis and Marty, the German shepherd.

"Yeah, I'd really like to meet your folks." An actual note of sincerity, as excitement once again kisses terror.

Now all I have to do is get through my date with the Judge. Apparently the Judge saw me at the orgy and asked for me. Sunny told me I wouldn't have to have sex with him. I made my "Oh, yeah, right!" face, but he swore there'd be no sex with the Judge. And it's a five-hundred-dollar job. This stopped me dead. Five hundred dollars.

"No sex? You swear?" I lean into the question.

"Ah swear on my dead pappy's asshole! The Judge, he don't go with no boys, but he likes to git hisseff roughed up a li'l bit. An' he's a big fan of yours."

Five hundred clams to rough up a judge? Big fan of mine? Sure, why not? Then I'll quit all this shit and move in with Kristy.

" 'Night, Mom," I soprano as I toodle off to beddybyes when I'm thirteen.

During the night my testicles drop like a couple of lode-stones in a bowl of pea soup.

"Good morning, Mother. Hope you slept well!" booms out of me in a breakfast baritone the next morning, and suddenly I'm fevered with curiosity, mad as a hatter with a hard-on.

Sex.

What goes in where with whom and how?

The Judge comes out of the bathroom in a judge's robe. Sunny told me he was a judge, but I didn't expect him to come out of the bathroom in his judge's robe. I'd arrived at the Griffith Park apartment about ten minutes ago, found the key under a loose brick, and let myself in as instructed. There was no one there, and I had a mini-mal panic seizure. G-men in closets. SWAT team swooping down and busting my ass. I scanned the room. Elegant and simple. Antique table, two chairs, and a Frenchish desk on which sat a manila envelope. Just like Sunny said. I relaxed. A little. A white envelope was hiding inside. I scooped it out carefully and opened it slowly. Inside were five naked hundred-dollar bills that make me safe and warm. They fit so nice in my pocket. Five hundred dollars for an hour. I *am* hot.

A typed note, folded in half, crouched in the envelope, containing explicit instructions involving me, the Judge (who referred to himself throughout as "The Judge"), and a metal-edged ruler.

How far I've come in my career, I thought, from telling women how beautiful they are while I'm naked to telling a Judge how horrible he is while he's naked.

White goo oozes from the eyes of the clerk who lurks behind the counter of the Pink Pussycat when I'm thirteen. One rotten tooth sits like a black plank in the middle of his cankerous cavern of a mouth. His head is too small for his body.

When I ask for change, hovering in the comfort of the Shadow, a deep wet eighteen-wheeler of a hack rumbles up the highway of the clerk's lungs, and he hands me four droopy, drooling quarters.

"Thank you," I chirp, cheery as a cherry popover.

The Pink Pussycat teems with heaps of steaming mags and sweaty videotapes. *Hot Pink Wet Virgin Slut Cheerleader Lesbo Nuns.* Loads of lone wolves with cigarette breath and damaged skin play pocket pool, ogle the magazines, and fondle the Plastic Love Dolls.

"Marilyn comes complete with silky hair. All organs are realistic in every detail. Heavy-duty vacuum bulb builds up amazing suction. Make her as skinny or as buxom as you want. Don't be fooled by cheap breakable imitations. Be the stud you always wanted to be."

I was instructed to burn the instructions and put the ashes in the sink. I liked that part. Gave it a real *Mission:*

Impossible feel. If I'm caught or killed the secretary will disavow any knowledge of my actions.

The matches waited by the sink next to the old-fashioned metal-edged ruler. The Judge doesn't miss a trick. Guess that's why he's the Judge. I lit a match and ignited the instructions. Puff of flame, smell of sulfur. I dropped it in the sink like a flaming dead Viking being floated out to sea.

I picked up the ruler with the cold metal edge, and it made a nice loud whack sound when I smacked it into my palm.

A muscle memory hit me, and *wham!* I was back in George Wallace Elementary School. My third-grade teacher, the ninety-seven-year-old Mrs. Bronte, the dreaded brontosaurus, all three-foot-nine of her, was dragging out the old metal-edged ruler to thrash some poor sucker's knuckles, the sixty-four eight-year-olds in my class smelling blood, silently wild with delight.

Fluorescent-pink signs shine like flaming flamingos in the Pink Pussycat, describing in a child's uneven scrawl the films being shown in each booth.

> *2 SLUTS WIT A STUD.*
>
> *2 STUDS AND A SLUT*
>
> *A STUD, A SLUT, AND A SHEPLAN PONEE.*

But I don't want all the bells and whistles. I'm thirteen, horny as a schoolgirl and nervous as a sailor, and I just want to see a normal guy and a normal gal doing what normal people do when they Do It. It never dawns on me that I might be in the wrong place to see anything like that.

The Judge is gray on gray, in all his robed glory, skin hanging flaccid cheek by jowl, dangling waddle wobbling over his collar, ushering a sour graveyard smell in with him.

As soon as I lay eyes on him I feel mean and hateful. I can see the Olde Bastard looking down from the bench with righteous condescension, telling me what a menace to society I am.

I slap the ruler hard into my hand, a loud *smack*, and it hurts, which helps, like Bruce Lee tasting his own blood. The Judge jumps, and that feels good.

"You're a miserable piece of shit, aren't you?" I stride right over to him all revved up *Clockwork Orange*–style, and I punch him knuckle on nose.

That's what I *want* to do. What I really do is stop my fist inches from the Judge's face, which registers high-voltage fright as he quivers in rapture and terror.

"Yes," he whimpers, "I need—"

"Shut up, bitch!"

I push him back into the wall, and he slumps with a thump. I tear the robe off him and shove him down. Guess what the Judge has on under his robes?

Diapers.

1 STUD, 1 SLUT, SOOPER HOT HOT HOT

That's about as normal as it's gonna get. The inside of the Pink Pussycat booth smells like an old moldy sperm sandwich. I slip a quivering quarter into the slick slot, and when a small screen flickers to life, a woman's face appears. She's cockeyed. One eye goes east, one goes west, one flies over the cuckoo's nest. She wears makeup buckwheat-pancake thick. A soundtrack of bad wackawacka guitar and synthesized drummachine wheezes under the sludgebucket basso profundo moan of a man loaded on testosterone.

"Oh baby. Give it to me, you nasty little baby. You love it, don't you, baby? Oh, baby, baby, baby."

She moans but no sound comes out. Then I hear a moan when her mouth isn't moving. It's out of kilter. Out of sync. Cockeyed.

She glances off camera, and you can almost hear some dictator director shouting:

"Act sexy!"

One eye darts back to the camera, while the other drifts off somewhere as she licks her lips and rolls her eyes. She's not sooper hot at all. She's sad in one eye and gone in the other.

Usually when an employer gets a bad haircut or wears an ugly tie, the employee doesn't get the opportunity to humiliate him or her. But that's what I'm getting paid for. I let loose a nice long sadistic laugh as I look at this sad gray Olde Bastard on his knees, with his flabby saggy tits, big pregnant cannonball gut, puddly thighs, and hunched shoulders grown wild with a nasty forest of white hairs.

In his diapers.

"Hey, wait a—" the Judge starts indignantly.

"Did I tell you to talk? No. You talk when I tell you to, you fat little prick—"

"Yes, I am, I'm a fat little prick," he dribbles.

"Shut the hell up, bitch!" I hiss, pissed, whacking him with the flat part of the ruler across the middle of his back, a howl yowling out of him as he bellyflops on the floor.

"Does your wife know you like to wear diapers? Do all the

lawyers and judges know you like to cum in your diapers? Answer me!"

"No," the Judge snivels.

"No 'sir,' bitch!" I snarl.

"No, sir . . ." the Judge whines.

His fear feeds me, and I gorge ravenously. But it's like stuffing yourself with day-old birthday cake that you know is gonna make you sick later.

"Put your hands out in front of you," I rumble.

This command comes with a smack of the ruler on his fat belly, accompanied by a tremendous slapping sound. The Judge averts his eyes like I'm the pope, and sticks his gray spotted hands out in front of him. I've got this rich pillar-of-society prick right where I want him.

In her left hand the cockeyed girl holds a plastic champagne glass, and in her right a veiny, blood-engorged wangdangdoodlehammer that she glances at sideways, like it might take a bite out of her cheek.

Then the screen goes dark. I desperately need to know what happens to my distressed porno princess, so I ram in another quarter, and there she is, exactly where I left her, licking her lips again, rolling her eyes back in her head like a tropical fish about to plunge into a coma, and winkling the wangdangdoodlehammer into the plastic champagne glass.

My femme fatale looks offscreen in a panic. "Do I have to?" flashes across her face. Apparently she does, cuz then she looks back at the camera, does her pseudosexy face again, and chugs the whole thing down.

Bottoms up!

"Shut your eyes!" I bark to the diapered Judge kneeling with his hands held in front of him. He closes them instantly. I like that. He's breathing hard and sweating like a fat old pig having sick sex.

I silently slide behind him, rear back, and smack him hard with the ruler on the pink bottom of his soul, catching his foot flush with another tremendous thwack that tingles deliciously all the way through my central nervous system.

The Judge tumbles like Humpty Dumpty off his wall, whimpermoaning in little rhythmic spasms. I plant my foot in the middle of his back and crush him into the beige carpet, where he quakes with the secret creepy excitement a Judge can only get from being trashed by a boy chicken he's paying five hundred dollars.

Who pumped their poison into this poor guy? I feel sorry for the Judge. One part of me wants to stop and try to make him feel better.

But I can't. This feels too good.

Looking like a sick kid who just swallowed her medicine, my pornbaby cocks one eye into the camera while the other wanders away forlorn. The unheard offscreen commandant orders her to smile, and as she snaps back, the east eye smiles sicklysweet, while the west eye looks like it's about to cry.

Sex? That's sex? Shocked and wobbly, I reel and teeter, jellykneed. I stumble into the supercool of the Pink Pussycat black light, lean against the booth to regroup, then stagger through the flaccid limp love beads, roll past the drooling troll behind the counter, and get ejaculated through the front door, where the blast of blinding white light brings reality rushing back like the four o'clock uptown express.

When my life flashes before my eyes this is one of the things I'll see: that beat-up cockeyed ghost of a girl flickering away.

The Judge moangroans loud now, bucking and thrashing, crying out somewhere between a wheeze and a sob. Watching this fat Olde Bastard busting his nut in his diapers makes my skin slink away in shame and my brain revolt. How did I end up doing this? That's it for me. I gotta get out.

The Judge finally stops and looks up at me. Seeing his ashen sicksad deathmask face makes my temperature drop thirty degrees, and I shiver the shiver of the damned. I grab my helmet, check my money, and mutter, "Later . . ."

Whatever.

16. Where Are My Keys?

You always hurt the one you love
The one you shouldn't hurt at all

—FISHER & ROBERTS

Easter morning I wake up with my head full of chain saws and out-of-tune violins, while my dead brain cells are getting a twenty-one-gun salute. My hovel has never looked so squalid. I have no memory of Saturday night after a tequila-drinking contest with a red bloated ex-sailor who had a tattoo of Popeye on his forearm he could make dance by wiggling his muscles. The drunker we got, the funnier Popeye danced.

Thank God my motorcycle helmet is on the floor near my bed. Thank God my head's not in the helmet, rolling down an off-ramp of the Hollywood Freeway.

I try to get up. Big mistake. Whole new levels of pain bells ring in my head, my chest, and all the way down to the balls of my feet. The effort overwhelms me, and I land back on the too-thin mattress that barely functions as my bed.

I manage to drag myself into the all-fours position, and pause here for quite some time, although time is particularly relative now, agony extending seconds like dripping hungover stopwatches. I'm exhausted and I haven't been awake five minutes.

Easter. Kristy. What time is it? Shit. I look for my miserable little clock, but I can't find it, and it hurts too much to keep looking.

Ever since the orgy I've felt compelled to hang at Immaculate Heart College playing Frisbee and Ping-Pong with people I don't even like just so I can be with other kids my age who aren't sex technicians. So Easter with Kristy's parents looms ahead like Mecca just past the Valley of Death, hope and longing lurking skittishly with the dread that they'll see me for the whore I am. And I've already created a waking nightmare for myself by sheepdipping my head in cheap liquor last night.

The phone rings. My first impulse is that it's Kristy, and I'm late. I'm supposed to be at her house at noon, and God knows what time it is. I rush, or try to get somewhere near the speed of rush, through the cold oatmeal I seem to be stuck in, still fully dressed in last night's alcohol-drenched nicotine-stenched clothing. Arid and parched, I cross the vast expense of living-room desert and throbbingly grab the phone.

"Hooo-ie, how you doin', bay-bay?"

It's Sunny. Of course. Who else would it be?

"I'm good, man, what time is it?" Sour's in my mouth, I need to pee and possibly shit. And shower. Soon.

"'Leven," Sunny coos.

I breathe easier. Got a little time.

"How you doin'?" manages to mutter out of me.

"Cool as a cucumber up a Eskimo's asshole."

I chuckle. Big mistake, as a cranial ache pulsates.

"Par-ty, bay-bay! Ah got me a new bonnet with awll the frills upon it, an' Ah'll be the finest fay-ree in the Easter Parade!"

I hear the drums beating the call of the wild.

My mom hurricanes around the house, fixing her huge bouffanty frosted helmethead, roasting beef, making tetties and Yorkshire puddings, preparing my brother and sister for presentation, straightening the house.

As a four-year-old I remember thinking how strange that is. To straighten the house. I see our crooked, crippled house, and my mother desperately trying to straighten it.

My mom's all sweetness and light as my dad gets home from work and we sit down for dinner. We say the grace we always say:

"God is great, God is good, and we thank him for our food."

I'm bothered by the fact that "good" and "food" don't rhyme.

"Thanks, man, but I got a date." I'm firm in my hungover resolve to choose life.

"Ohhhh, you gotchoo some nice coed pussy—well, ain't that sweet? Bring 'er awn over." Sunny coos.

Kristy, these are my wacky child-prostitute friends. Cruella, say hello to my lady.

"Naw, I don't think so." I'm firm.

"Well, hell, cum awn by when you done gittin' pussy-whupped, and you can have some of my chocolate aiggs." Sunny almost makes you believe life really is a cabaret.

"In your dreams, baby."

"They'z gonna be some Easter bunnies with some tight li'l baskets for your ass," Sunny hisses hypnotically.

Visions of 3-D overflowing with freaks and friends and a sweet baby for me dance like sugarplum fairies in the pin of my head.

Now wait a minute, hold on one goddam second here, you are not jumping down that hole. Barbecue, watermelon, cornonthecob, Mom, Dad, Dog, Sis, Kristy's Easter Sunday, end of discussion, case closed.

This is your ticket out of all the shit, boy.

"Thanks, man, but I, you know, got this thing I gotta do . . ." That's as firm as it gets for me right now.

"Aw-ite, but just in case you change your mind, Ah'll keep a bunny warm for ya. Oh, an' Ah got a real nice job for you Mundee night—easy money, boy, five hunnert. An awll you gotta do is act natch-ally."

Sunny's the master carrot dangler.

I start to turn the job down. The words form in my brain and travel all the way to my mouth. I just can't get them to come out.

"You hear me, boy?"

This is not the response Sunny wants.

"Yeah, absolutely. My roommate was just talkin' to me— *Yeah, I'll take care of that*—uh, sure, job Monday, that's cool, five hundred, yeah . . ." I'm shaky, I can hear I am.

"You aw-ite, boy? Somethin' botherin' you?" Sunny sounds like a fight doctor whose prizefighter has just taken a shot to the head.

"No, I'm cool," I lie. Ever since the Judge I've been snappish, brittled, fraying, ready to bite someone's head off. Not cool at all.

"An' Ah almost forgot, that goil Jade's gonna be here tonight, she told me she like to git together whichew." Sunny knows where every button is, and he's pushing them all.

Jade invades my brain and I feel her in my belly. Jade in a slinky kinky dress, with those sleepy almond eyes dancing to the music in her head.

No. You're going to Kristy's parents', you're going to be the perfect boyfriend, and I don't wanna hear one more word about it.

"Tell her to give me a call."

I'm proud I could say no.

"Aw-ite, well, good luck, boy, you gonna need it. An' remember, when you git tired of awll that prissy pussy, you come awn down, and we tighten your wig for ya."

Sunny chuckles. Then he's gone.

Something's off at the dinner table. Way off. Even as a four-year-old I can see that. My mom's pissed my dad off, and there's an edgy terror to everything. He's not speaking to her. He babbles on about how much wind he broke at work, but not a word to my mother.

Not one word. Not a nod or a wink. Nothing.

My mom wrings her hands and itches the psoriasis breaking out in red patches of anger on her elbows and scalp.

My head hurts worse when I hang up the phone. Who am I kidding? Kristy's folks are gonna take one look at me and give me the bum's rush. I'm going to Sunny's.

No. Stop. Get in the shower, get your shit together, walk out the door, get on the bike, go over to Kristy's parents' house, and nicely be her Easter boy.

But as I shower and dress in my blue button-up shirt and my green corduroys, I can't get around the fact that getting dolled up and acting normal for Kristy and her folks sounds like dental surgery. Her parents are probably uptight prigs. Hey, I don't have to perform like some trained monkey for Kristy and her dumbass daddy and mommy.

Whereas if I go to Sunny's I can just be a whore.

And Jade is gonna be there. Jade asked about me.

There are moments in all our lives when we're faced with choices that make us who we will become. This is now for me.

Kristy vs. Sunny.

But first, before I choose anything, I must have a nervous breakdown. And to do this I need something to focus all my fury on.

My keys.

My dad doesn't speak to my mom for three weeks. Just cuts her off cold. Breakfast, dinner, weekends. Will not speak to her.

The message is clear. This is what a husband does when he's mad at his wife: deepfreeze her.

The reason my dad wouldn't speak to my mom for three weeks, I found out recently, was that she'd had a washing-machine accident and flooded the basement, causing some water damage.

Where are my keys?

"Does Braddy love Mommy?"

Flabby Judge wobbles in grotesque rapture.

Tinkerbell floats away forever.

Change the record, Cheesehead.

It's getting so I can't find a happy record with a beat you can dance to. All my records seem to be soundtracks to my personal horror movies.

I look in the mirror and a harrowed haunted teenager looks back at me. I'm my own portrait of Dorian Gray, and my sins stare me right in the face.

I can do this. Go to Kristy's. Get myself out of this nasty life. Maybe her Old Man can get me a job. Move in with her. Yeah, that's a good thought to hold on to.

Now all I have to do is find my keys.

In the pocket of my blue-jean jacket, there are no keys. The old roadkill door I found and transformed into a desk by propping it up on plastic milk crates is so overflowing with detritus I can't even see any tabletopdoor: pens stolen from banks with the chains still attached; little bits of paper with names, numbers, song lyrics, philosophical treatises, rants and raves; a leftover cake container and a dead pint of ice cream; soiled coins, dark wadded dollar bills; a pair of glasses with eyeballs attached to slinkies that shake around and wobble when you put them on and move your head.

But no keys. Shit. I always leave my keys here. This is where I leave my keys. Damn. Look at all this pitiful useless shit. This is my life?

Stop. Where was the last place I saw the keys? Actually, I have no memory of my keys. Do I even have keys?

Stop. Keys. A pair of shorts on the floor. Maybe they're in there. Loose change, pack of matches, Tootsie Pop.

No keys. Shit!

In the living room I look on the Salvation Army foldable card table, and in plastic milk crates that are doing time as end tables.

No keys.

Into the bathroom. Maybe I swallowed them and they came out when I took a shit.

No keys.

Not in the shower. Not on the floor. Not under the rug.

Into the kitchen. Where are my keys? Keys, keys, keys. Not on the floor. Not in the sink. Under the sink? Who knows, I was stone drunk, it's possible. I bend down, open the cabinets, and poke my head into the dark under there, soaking in the Clorox ammonia potpourri.

No keys.

I back out.

Bam! My head hits the sink with a thick thud.

Motherbitchdickfacebastardpussyassshit!!!

The head was just starting to feel normal after being in the Battle of the Bulge all morning, but the hurt bounces around inside now like a pinball of pain—

TILT! TILT! TILT!

I'm a hopping madman holding my throbbing skull. I punch the kitchen wall with my fist. I expect to break a hole in it with my fury, but it doesn't give at all, and a whole new pain takes a bite out of my knuckles, cranking up the volume knob in my head. The hurt humps its way up my arm and into my spine before it rattles down into my ass.

"Sonofadogsuckingdickwadbitch!!!"

Totally out of my mind, I smashmouth off the walls down the hall, pissed-off radiating out of me like plutonium.

Where are my goddam keys?

Suddenly I'm back in my hovel, picking up fistfuls of desktop crap and flinging them against my stained rug walls as hard as I can, scattering my worthless crap to the four corners of my miserable little universe.

Splat! Splatter! Whack!

Then I pick up my shitty granddad roadkill chair, raise it over my head, and smash it down as hard as I can. It hits the floor with a satisfying crack, and explodes, transforming instantly into kindling.

It's unclear how smashing my chair was going to help me find my keys, but at the time it seems like exactly the right thing to do. Plus it feels so good.

I pick up the doortabletop, hold it over my head, and ram it hard into a hanging mirror, and oh, man, that bastard shatters into a million jagged sharp shards that rain down like confetti in hell.

The smashed glass makes me take a step back. I take it all in. My little hellhole looks like it threw itself on a grenade to save the rest of the platoon. When I get my breath back I collapse onto my nasty slagheap mattress, horrified and impressed, a postcoital wrungout calm balming over me.

Hey, maybe I should have a wee little nap.

Then I'm asleep.

I wake up floating in the debris of my life. The thought of even calling Kristy now makes me shrivel like a spider on a hot plate, and in one swift instant I dismiss the thought.

When I realize I no longer have to go to Kristy's, my head clears like the midday fog off the Golden Gate Bridge, revealing a beauty of a bluesky day, and I have a burst of energy as my hangover vacates the premises.

I straighten and organize my room slowly, reconstructing my deconstructed self by bringing order to the chaos that is my room.

When I'm done I fondle my cash stash like a long-lost lover. Maybe I should ask Sunny if he wants to go in together, get a nice place, start a serious business where we can make the Really Big Money, have a nice room of my own, fix it up, help get Jade out of the junk jungle, and be one big happy family.

I can see it so clearly.

I've done something bad. I can't now remember what it was, but it was bad. My father grips the steering wheel of the van, his gnarly knuckles snow white, jaw sprung shut like a bear trap.

"Dad, I'm sorry . . .

"I'm sorry, Dad . . .

"Are you mad, Dad?

"Dad, are you mad?

"Are you mad, Dad?

"Dad, are you mad?

"I'm sorry, Dad . . ."

I want to quit whinging, but the more Silence he unleashes on me, the more I become a miserable little stain on the passenger seat.

I ride my bike to 3-D through a sweet Easter Sunday zephyr. It's a peaceful afternoon. Or maybe it's me that's peaceful.

I don't see Kristy's pissed-off, embarrassed humiliation. I

don't see her kicking herself for picking me. I don't see her explaining where I am to her parents while they shake their disapproving heads. I don't see any of that.

As I toodle down Hollywood Boulevard into the seedy loins of Tinsel Town, I can practically hear the Beach Boys singing about all the funfunfun we're gonna have till our Daddy takes the T-Bird away, while the stragglers push their grocery baskets full of everything they own, like they're hunting for eggs, talking to their own Harvey Easter Bunny.

Into 3-D I stride like a samurai chicken coming in from the cold of the hero's road, pushing that big huge rock up that big huge mountain. Sunny's is jive jumpin' buzz humpin' packed to the gills, tits to the wind and balls to the wall, as I get bumps from my freaks and pecks from my chickens.

"Hooo-ie, boy, Ah knew you couldn't stay away."

Sunny's decked out in a green sparkly dress with dangly bangles and fake hooters, topped off by a giant Easter bonnet with an egg-filled Easter basket attached.

You can't help but laugh. So I laugh. And with that the yoke of my load lifts. I'm home with my homies, celebrated for my winning personality, lack of boundaries, and nice bum.

Sunny kisses me on both cheeks. I low-five Horse, kiss Cruella, and case the joint. Redheads, deadheads, blondies, brownies, blackies, lackies, hot fudge and cherries, fatties and thinnies, and lots of old faces on young bodies.

Me, I'm looking for some Jade.

"Is she here?" I say, way too eager.

"Hold your water, boy. You gotta eat foist." Sunny yanks me toward the kitchen and fixes me a plate of sweet potatoes, black-eyed peas, biscuits, and a couple slabs of ham, pink pig wafting succulent up into my bottomless pit.

When all the food is gone from my plate, Sunny dragqueens me into the living room, through the messy mass of Easter madness. There on the couch sits a girl in a one-piece bathing suit, fluffy bunny tail, and big floppy ears attached to a barrette clinging hard to her head. She carries an Easter basket full of little airline liquor bottles; marijuana cigarettes; yellow red green blue and teal pills; a sheet with little Mickey Mouses smiling LSDishly from it; and some gray magic mushrooms. The girl is kinda funny looking, but cute, Italian skin, crazy curly brown hair, a goofy offcentric nose, chipmunk cheeks, extra-thick milkshake lips, eyes the color of a putting green, and chubbly wubbly, weebly wobbly flesh jiggling from under her one-piece, with an overflowing cornucopia of décolletage.

"This here is Honey Bunny." Sunny nods to me, then winks to her. "This here's the boy I'ze telling you about. You do everything he says, and Ah mean *evva-ree-thing*." He bugs his eyes and she giggles, which makes her jiggle like a bowlful of royal sex jelly.

"Hi, Honey Bunny." I smile as Sunny spangles away.

"Happy Easter," she replies, like a silly little kid playing dress-up.

"I'm always confused about Easter. Is that where Jesus comes back from the dead, peeks his head up from a hole in the ground, and if he sees his shadow, he knows winter's over?" I go right to the A material.

"That's funny . . . did you just make that up?" She stares at me hard and smiles soft. Now she looks like she's a student in an accelerated learning class at Lyndon Baines Johnson High School.

"No, actually, I have a staff of writers working round-the-clock just churning the shit out." After my deadpan I sneak in a little smile to let her know I'm funning her.

She laughs smart, intelligence burning in her eyes. Comedy is what separates us from the beasts. How did a girl like her end up an Easter Bunny toting intoxicating eggs in Sunny's web? We shall have to get to the bottom of this bunny tale.

As I slam a small Jack I scan the room, surveying the 3-D grid for Jade. Where oh where can my baby be? She's at her mom and dad's house on Easter with her dog Marty, trying not to think about what a piece of shit I am.

Change that record, lad.

It's so easy at Sunny's to change any record. There's so much interesting music here. It doesn't take much coaxing to get Honey Bunny to spill her rabbit guts. Mother died of breast cancer, alcoholic father "did things" to her and her little sister, so she told her teacher, who told the authorities, who arrested the father, who got sent to prison; the father's family disowned her and her sister, then the mother's parents got hit by a truck driven by some guy who's blind drunk, then she and the sister got shipped to some home for kids who have nothing and no one, where they waited for a kindly foster family to rescue them from their misery; only while they're waiting, some of the caretakers "did things" to her and her little sister; so she told the authorities, who accused her of being a troublemaker, and punished her and her sister until they ran away and made it to L.A.; then she got in a big fight with her little sister about Sunny and money and being a bunny chicken, and her sister took off and she's worried sick that her sister is dead, "or worse," and she wants to start working for Sunny, cuz she's dead broke, "no kidding, we're totally broke, you have no idea!" She heard the work was pretty good, and if you do it right you can make a lot of money, sure beats flipping burgers— "I want to go to Harvard," that's her dream, be a lawyer, bust scumbags who do bad things to girls. "It's not that horrible, is it, the work?" She looks at me like a hungry motherless pup.

"Better than a sharp stick in the eye." I smile. I tell her to get a specialty, save her money, then get the hell out.

"That's what I'm doing," I hear myself say.

Is that what I'm doing?

Then why am I here instead of at Kristy's parents?

"Thanks." She takes my hand and kisses it, like we're in some medieval fairy tale, and suddenly I'm warm toasty tasty with the possibilities of this bundle of desperate budding vulnerable Honey Bunny sexuality.

I'm thirteen, home alone.

I've recently discovered how much fun it is sliding my hand up and down my penis. Gwenyvere bounds into my room. She's English, adorably happy and sweet, complete with big beautiful lovey eyes.

Suddenly she's using me as her human lollipop, and before you can say lickety-split, my lollapalooza is cabooming all over the place.

Gwenyvere seems to really enjoy it.

Frankly, so do I.

I never had a sense of sexual right and wrong.

As far as I'm concerned, we are just a boy and a dog enjoying each other's company.

"**What's** your real name?" I ask Honey Bunny.

I almost never ask. Usually I don't want to know. But I like her. She's warm and smart and cuddly and funny and sexy, and it would be such fun to bury my face in her soft pillow. And I bet she could make a lot of money. Maybe we can find her sister and get her working, too, get a nice place together the three of us, and kiss one another's hands.

"Sophie," says Honey Bunny.

She looks exactly like a Sophie. I want to protect this girl. And destroy her. Just like I'm doing to myself. Just like I'm doing to Kristy.

I'm just about to pop the "why don't we go back to my groovy clean pad" question to Sophie when who should come waltzing in?

Sophie's sister, that's who, looking like she's being followed by somebody who wants to "do things" to her.

Sophie shrieks so loud the party stops. She and her sister grab each other like the world's about to come to an end and this is the last thing they want to be doing before the Apocalypse.

After the assembled let out a collective sigh, roll their eyes, and make their catty remarks, the party comes back to life, and I watch the little sister be swallowed up in the big sister.

Sophie takes off her bunny accoutrements, and the sisters whisper how they'll never leave each other ever again. Little sister's in dirty white overalls, longer and leaner than Sophie, but clearly from the same gene pool.

Hey, maybe I *can* have sex with them. Maybe the gods are smiling on me after all.

Sophie looks like a big sister now, so sweet and easy and full of comfort. I see me and my little brother the night of the Great Pea Scandal of '64, just the two of us in our beds, me and my little brother, who'll always love each other no matter what. I miss him so much.

Sophie brings her little sister over to meet me. Mary Beth. Sophie tells me Mary Beth called a cousin in Phoenix and he's wiring them money so they can go live with him till they figure out what to do next.

It's remarkable to watch this happen right in front of my eyes. I imagine them telling their kids and grandkids about this.

How they got out just in the nick of time.

17. The Walrus

I am not a slut, though I thank the gods
I am foul.

—SHAKESPEARE

On the last day I am a chicken, the phone rings.

"Hey, boy." There's no *et toi* in Sunny's voice.

"What's the matter?" My ass starts to hurt.

"Got some bad news. Call jest come in. Jade . . . she's dead. Last night, she got herself beat up. Ah'm sorry, Ah know you had a thing for her, so Ah wanted you to hear it from me," Sunny says soft.

My heart stops, and then sinks with me as I collapse onto the couch. I see Jade dancing to that tune playing in her head, half geisha half trained killer. Big tears suddenly fill my eyes, and I cover my face with my hands to stop them from coming out. They're so close, right there, waiting. But I won't let them out.

"You aw-ite, boy?"

Sunny brings me back to the land of the living.

"You sure you wanna woik tonight? Ya wanna cancel?" Sunny shifts seamlessly from concerned family member to calculated business manager.

I shut it down, pack it up, and store it away.

"No, I'm cool. It's sad, but like you said, she was a messed-up girl. Hey, five hundred bucks is five hundred bucks, right?"

"Yeah, aw-ite, well . . . come by when you done."

And then Sunny is gone.

Jade was probably junked up, did something stupid, got herself whacked or jacked or smacked.

Not my fault. Not my problem.

Whatever.

In the backyard my father calls Juliette, and she bounds over happily, ready to love and be loved. She's French and very refined, by far the most functional member of our family unit.

As she gets to the picnic table, she makes eye contact with my dad, and her blood runs cold, tail snapping up hard between her legs, everything shrinking up as she tries to slink away unnoticed.

But there's no escape for Juliette.

My dad grabs her, one hand on the collar, one under the belly, plops her down on the picnic table covered with a stained sheet, fires up the old sheep shearer, and begins scalping the defenseless Juliette, who looks around with the biggest, saddest, how-much-is-that-doggy-in-the-window eyes, like some captured French freedom fighter pleading, " 'Elp me, s'il vous plaît!"

We can't help ourselves, how can we help her?

My old man shaves and shaves the whimpering Juliette until there's five pounds of curly black pubes on the old stained sheet, and she's barebuttbald.

Juliette spends the next weeks hiding under tables, chairs,

and beds, ashamed to face the humiliating heckling of the neighborhood dogs.

I'll soon know how she feels.

Old, stuffy, and puffing a pipe with a mustache, he looks like a walrus in a bloodred smoking jacket. He wears no slippers, and his long narrow feet are covered by skin so translucent you can see pale blue rivers running under it. He sits too erect, trying to suck in his gut, like he's posing for a portrait with an invisible javelin stuck up his ass. His pad's neat as a pin with a cleaning disorder, and lavishly appointed with rich rugs, gaudy goblets, and kitschy knickknacks. A scratchy 78 of Judy Garland doing "Happiness Is a Thing Called Joe" plays on an old-time Victrola. He looks like he's constructed his life so he's the star of his own Noël Coward play.

I can't wait to wipe that thin grin off his smug mug.

No instructions have been given. He did hand me five hundred dollars, but when I took it he held on to it too long, so I had to yank it out of his hand. That made me mad. I gotta tell Sunny. From now on, I want an envelope, on the table, no questions asked.

I'm gunslinger calm, but my blood is bubbling, and a brain-fever so severe I can barely see straight rages within.

And I'm focusing my beam right at this old rich stuck-up queen with a walrus mustache.

It's a week after my dad scalped Juliette the dog, and the night before our family's going on vacation with my cousins. My dad lines us all up: me, my brother, and my two cousins, while

Juliette sneaks furtive glances from around the corner, reliving her horror, wondering if she'll be next.

My father grabs my nine-year-old head with one hand, thumb and forefinger squeezing temples, the sheepshearer buzz surround-sounding me, loud and louder, scraping like nails across the blackboard of my jangling nerves till I'm vibrating with the exact same frequency, as my dad buzzcuts his way across the quivering egg of my head.

I see Jade with a bullet hole in her head.

Change the record.

I look around the Walrus's room for some life jacket to jack into, and I spot a cheesy figurine of Peter Pan, all in green, head to toe, with those pointy little green shoes, and that Puck grin.

Tinkerbell. Is she dead, too?

Change the record.

The Walrus drones on about how he saw me at the orgy, and how he knew he had to have me. Have me? A wolverine snarl curls inside me. I think you're confused. It's me who's gonna have you.

He wants to know if I remember him from the orgy. He was dressed as a satyr, the mythological half man half beast who embodies raw sexuality and is hung like a horse.

He wants me to remember him, so I pretend I remember him. Tell him what a great costume he had, how I believe we've lost sight of our animal selves as we get more civilized, and that I wasn't surprised he was hung like a horse.

He likes it. Which is why I say it. But it's getting warm in here. This trick seems to be under the mistaken impression that some kind of sexysex is about to happen here. We'll have to disabuse him of that notion quickly. And he's always playing with that mustache. Twirling it, stroking it, massaging it. Makes me want to slap it right off his face, and watch the red rose of a bruise bloom on his cheek.

Almost like he's reading my mind, he shoots me a look like he thinks he's a real naughty boy. I give him back some cold hard steel.

Let the games begin.

The heavymetal sheapshearer is hot on my skull, I smell the warm oily machineness, and I hear my hairs scream out as they're shorn short, shocked, trickling prickly and itchy, shivering down my back.

As my dad mows the yard of my head, the grip of his vise tightens around my temples, and I absorb it into me like a new computer with an empty hard drive, his fingers plugged into the skuzzy ports on either side of my head, filling me with an angry silent virus.

And then we're barebuttbald, just like Juliette.

Everyone's extra quiet at bedtime, none of the jocularity and staying-up-late behavior that characterizes our group dynamic, no teasing about how ugly we look, cuz we all look ugly, little Sampsons sapped of our strength.

The Walrus wants me to come over to him. I still don't know what he wants. I don't like that. I don't like him.

Jade impaled on a junkspike.

I want to plant my fist in the garden of his face. I walk over to him hard with my fist closed tight, and I move to smack him, just a little move, but full of all the violence that's hiding under my kitchen table.

He cringes and gets hard at the same time.

"Wait a second, sonny, I've gotta get in the mood," the Walrus whines.

I ain't your sonny, and I don't give a damn about your mood. I'm ready to go right here, right now.

The Walrus slowly opens up his smoking jacket, with an "aren't I a naughty boy?" look.

Under his smoking blood-colored jacket is a black leather bustier with a bulletbra.

The Walrus doesn't look like a naughty boy to me. He seems like somebody I want to watch double up in agony. But he wants me to tell him what a naughty boy he is, I know that, so I swallow my self again and add another bone to the cauldron bubbling inside me.

"Wow," I say, "that is some crazy shit."

He pats a spot on the love seat. He wants me to sit down next to him. Against every impulse in my being, I sit, getting more queased with the lingering suspicion that this nasty Olde Bastard is expecting some kind of sex. A thin line of sweat heads south from under my arm.

"Hey, man, let's get one thing straight here. We're not doing any . . . sex thing here, you understand that, right?"

He smiles like a community theater player trying to portray a suave gadabouttown, and the sheer smarm of him almost knocks me off the chair.

"Yes, I guess we need to get it . . . 'straight.' " He's thrilled with himself for being so damn witty. "No, I have a wonderful itinerary planned for us, but you will not be required to do any . . . 'sex things.' "

The mocking nags at my guts. He thinks he's smarter than me. He thinks he's better than me. Not for long, my friend.

The Walrus wants me to threaten to have my way with him with brute force.

"But first, I want to get in the mood." The Walrus leers like a loungelizard in a bulletbra.

He puts his hand on my head, which makes the junk jump in my stomach, and shrivels my balls. He pulls my head toward him and rests it on the cold leather of the chest of the bulletbra.

The thin sheet of ice is cracking all around me.

Barebuttbald and nine, I finally arrive with my family for our vacation on the Florida shore. We spend our first day cavorting on the beach under the torrent of tropical sun. I keep feeling like my head's too hot. I try to tell a grown-up, but I'm shushed. That night, all the boys complain about how hot their heads are.

Sun poisoning of the scalp. That's what we got. Painful puffing pussing and peeling follow. Worst of all, we have to wear these dumbass floppy golf hats like doddering codgers.

After that I have a special relationship with Juliette. She shoots me meaningful glances from time to time. I nod knowingly. We're members of the Barebuttbald Club.

I smell the leather. I see the Walrus manipulating himself under his silky pajama bottom.

Change the record.

Jade with empty eyes, not dancing anymore.

I feel a rhythmic tug on my head as my long hair hangs in my face, prickly on my cheek, and I hear a sucking sound that matches the pulls on my head. I strain to see what's being sucked on my skull. From the extreme corner of my sight line I spot the Walrus's face, tilted back, eyes rolled up so only the runny egg whites of his raptured eyes are showing.

The Walrus has my hair in his mouth.

And he's sucking on it.

The Walrus is sucking on my head.

Something all the way inside of me pops, and a beast is unleashed from my belly, rocketing me to my feet, my hair clumped and wet with Walrus spittle.

"What the hell is wrong with you, asshole?!" I roar like a prehistoric monster.

"Now, wait a minute! I'm not—"

"No, *you* wait a minute, bitch!"

I slap him across the cheek. *Whack!* Loud. Skin on skin. That's good.

"Please!"

Worry wades across the face of the Walrus as he pleads and bleeds from the corner of his mouth. At this moment he realizes he's made a dangerous mistake inviting me into his parlor to play his little reindeer games.

The scare coming out of him makes me high.

"Shut up, punk!"

I pick up his Cowardly Lion statuette and throw it as hard as I can against the wall, where it shatters into a galaxy of tiny little scared lion pieces. Then I throw a fancy painted rock egg thing through his glass cabinet. He screams, and I reward him with a knuckled backhanded rap upside his head, which whips backward as he's jettisoned off the love seat to the plushy rug, while I feel more alive than I have in a long time. This one's for Jade, bastard! I rear my foot back and let fly, making solid contact with his stomach, his guts rocking backward as his breath disappears. The Walrus shakes on the floor, wheezing, fetal, looking up at me with a silent plea for sanity.

I pick up a Mae West–shaped lamp with two bulbs for breasts and fling it into a mirror, tit bulbs and shiny shattered platinum hair shooting everywhere.

There's a long lamp by a chair, six feet and skinny, with a heavymetal bottom base. I see myself raising it over my head and bringing it down on Walrus skull. I raise it high and it's heavy, perfectly weighted, the ideal tool for the job of cracking this Walrus like a coconut and watching the brainmilk drain out. I stalk toward him, fury blasting out of me like a fire-and-brimstone preacher.

The Walrus has wet his silk pajamas. I feel kind of bad for the guy. He just wanted a little slap and tickle. Not this hurricane of pain.

But I can't stop myself.

I bring that metalheaded pole flinging down with all my might, but instead of Walrus head I smash glass table, shards shooting and spitting.

TV. Yes. Next I swing that lampclub like it's a Big Bertha and I'm bombing the screen straight down the fairway. Smoke and sparks zip around like an electrical storm in a lighted globe.

I'm hot sweaty and breathy, having violence orgasms as I shatter my way through the Walrus's life.

I stalk back over to the Walrus, who's muttering, "Please, please, please . . ."

"Wanna suck on my hair again, you piece of shit?" The hate

flows from me as I dance with the devil's snake, leading hordes of Huns over the horizon to splay women and eat children.

Jade gagged with a plastic bag over her head.

I reach down slow, grab his rug, rip it off his head, and shove it into his mouth.

"How's that taste? Isn't that sexy?"

Then I rear back and pop him right in the nose. I always wanted to do that. You see it so much in the movies and it looks so cool. But in real life it's not nearly that good. It hurts the hell out of my knuckles. It does make a nice sound, though, that thwack of bone hard on bone.

Walrus's head drives back into the wall behind it with a thick thud.

I stormtrooper all over his pad, smashing thrashing and trashing, then I move back in, jazzed with madness. I squat on my haunches, and lean down like his face is the camera and I'm going in for my extreme close-up.

"If you tell Sunny or anybody else about this I'm gonna come back and finish you off, you understand me?"

No response.

The Walrus isn't moving. I shake him. Nothing.

"Hey, you all right?"

No response.

Now I'm scared. I see crime-scene photos of the fallen Walrus, his pristine apartment looking like Dresden after the bombing. Oh, shit, what have I done? I put my hand in front of his mouth. The Walrus is still breathing.

Walking away as fast as I can, I raise my defense shields to stop the raw rank fear that's trying to pin me on the bed and slam its way inside me.

I'm playing ball with the older neighborhood boys when I'm five. Somebody throws the ball over my head and it rolls into the yard next door, where there's an old mean German shepherd who's been chained to a pole for about a hundred years.

I see the white ball sitting in the green grass. When I crawl through the opening in the fence and reach down to grab the ball, I hear a metallic snap of a chain breaking. I look up and the German shepherd is flying at me, giant teeth bared, hungry for my flesh. I move at the last second, and the dog's mouth chomps onto my thigh, inches from my little penis.

I scream, and the whole neighborhood comes rushing.

I speedwalk to my bike, fingering my pager, my busted-up knuckle hurting like hell. I see cops swarming the Walrus pad with dogs, dusting for fingerprints, scouring every inch of the place for proof that it was me. Front page of the *L.A. Times* with a big picture of me being dragged away in handcuffs: BOY HOOKER BUSTED. My mom and dad in court, disgraced, my head bowed in shame, condemned by the Judge I abused as a symbol of everything that's wrong with America. Kristy and her parents in the back shaking their head. Waking up in prison with a tall SEXY man all over me.

Change the record nownownow!

A plan. I need a plan. I could keep driving until I get to an Indian reservation and live there. Go to Alaska and work on the pipeline. Lots of good work for a handy guy on the pipeline. Go to Mexico. Got enough money to live like a king on the beach, get a little señorita who cooks my meals and keeps me happy.

I drive past my street, but I don't go down it. Hordes of feds and G-men are probably going through my stuff, searching for the piece of evidence that's gonna send me to the stripy hole where I shall suffer the rest of my days.

Oh, shit, what's Sunny gonna think? I've been avoiding this thought, but now it bores full force into me. To hell with that bastard pimp. I'll turn him in. Hey, if I'm going down, I'm taking everybody down with me. What am I thinking? Those Hollywood Employment Agency bastards are killers. They will seriously kill you.

Hold everything. In my rearview mirror is a cop. He's giving me the hardcore five-oh eyeball. Or am I just feeling the eyeball? No idea. I turn down Vine. He follows me. Oh shit, I gotta hot copper on my tail. I come within a whisper on a whisker of gunning it, and making that bastard eat my dust as I high-speed-chase away from the LAPD on the six o'clock news.

But I stick steady, turn off onto a side street, take another fast turn, and lose him. I say "lose," but I guess technically you can't lose somebody who's not actually following you.

A plan, a plan, I need a plan.

Suddenly I have a true mystic vision.

Kristy.

I'll come clean, I'll make it up to her, and this time I'll be really good.

Then I feel my pager, hard cold and black in my pocket. This is the source of all the evil in my life. I slam on my brakes. I hop off my bike. I take the pager from my pocket, and slowly I raise it over my head.

The pager is hard cold and black in my hand as a righteous rush floods me.

I will break the curse of the chicken.

I slam my arm down as fast as I can.

Smash!

When the pager hits the pavement it bursts into a million cold hard black pieces, flying all over Hollywood Boulevard.

Free at last. Free at last.

Staring at the guts of my pager spread out all over the stars, I feel like a hero who's just killed the Jabberwocky and freed his people.

I am a chicken no more.

18. Ask

When the end comes I know they'll say
just a gigolo, life goes on without me.

—Julius Brammer, translated by
Irving Caesar

My busted-up knuckle hurts like hell, but I have no pager to finger as I park my bike and pull it up onto its stand quiet. It's dark and I'm animal aware of every sound on this little Hollywood side street. So this is what it feels like to be on the FBI Ten Most Wanted list. Someone's lurking behind every tree, about to slam around every corner, bounce out of every fake utility truck to bust my shit. *Breathe.* I wish I had a gun. I wonder where I can get a gun. Sunny'll know. Oh, shit, Sunny. He's gonna hate me now. After everything he did for me, I jacked him right where he lives. Hey, he deserves it.

Whatever.

Suddenly a car pulls up fast and parks about twenty feet away, on the same side of the street as me. I duck behind the side of a building. A couple of clean-looking guys get out quick, looking like Hollywood Employment Agency–hired goons come to rough me up and down. They're walking toward me. One of them reaches in his coat pocket for a gun. Oh, shit. I start to make a mad dash for it when he pulls out his keys. No gun. The only gun is in my head, and it's loaded and cocked, my own finger slowly squeezing the trigger.

Got to get ahold of myself. The Walrus splayed out on the floor. How did this happen to me? No, this didn't happen to me. I made it happen. But I didn't want to leave home. It's not my fault my father's having a nervous breakdown. It's not my fault my mother buggered off with her lover and didn't invite me along. Is that my fault? Hell, no.

Whatever.

The Walrus just got a little more punishment than he paid for. And on the bright side, he did learn a valuable lesson about hiring troubled youth to abuse him. Maybe this asswhupping'll turn his life around and make him a productive member of society. Hell, I probably did the guy a favor. And besides, who's he gonna tell? The cops? What's he gonna say? That he paid a chicken to rough him up and things got a little out of hand? I don't think so.

I will confess to my girl. I will baptize myself in the holy water of Kristy.

I walk behind the building to her little bungalow. I knock on her door. No answer. I have no Plan B. Maybe I'll just wait here until she comes home. Knock again. No answer. Shit.

I sit down on her stoop, prepared to wait for the rest of my life if necessary. But just as I settle in on her stoop, the door opens.

I look up. It's Kristy. God, I like this girl.

She doesn't see anyone at her door. She's confused. She wasn't expecting anyone, heard two knocks, and no one is there.

Guilt punches me in the chest. Why did I betray her? That

was a terrible thing to do. Only a terrible person would do something like that. If I'd just done the right thing I wouldn't have gone on that job with the Walrus. Wouldn't have pummeled that innocent pervert.

If ifs and ands were pots and pans, beggars would be kings. My mother used to say that.

Kristy feels someone staring at her, looks down, and when she sees it's me, her whole face tightens and darkens and hardens.

A wasp of shame stings me.

My mom endures the sixties as hausfrau, and she's determined not to miss the seventies doing laundry and cooking for a man who's not quite there.

At this time the Women's Movement is rearing its Sapphic head and roaring in all its glory. Consciousnesses are being raised willy-nilly, vaginas examined in mirrors, and bras burned in every city, 'burb, and village.

Our Bodies, Ourselves starts making the rounds in our house. We're all free to be you and me. Mommies are people, people with feelings.

It's all right to cry.

"What do you want?" A glacial cold snap sweeps down from Kristy and chills my blood. She used to look at me so nice.

"Please, Kristy, I'm sorry, I really am. I'm so sorry. Just give me five minutes. Please . . ." This is where I, master apologist, must begin.

"No, I don't think so." Kristy is unmoved.

"Please, I'm begging you, just give me five minutes . . . Kristy I'm desperate, please. I'm *so* sorry . . ." I plunge into full-frontal grovel.

A huge sadness rushes up me, and the tears are there again, only this time I don't stop them. I don't remember crying in front of someone my own age before, but I want back in so bad, I'm willing to walk a trail of tears to get there. My eyes get fuller and fuller, like udders that need to be milked. Then two waterfalls wash down the rock of my face, as I slowly empty.

Something moves in Kristy. She's not ready to let me back, but her good sweet heart is feeling me.

"Kristy, something really terrible happened to me, something I can't tell anybody about. But I want to tell you, so you'll understand. Please, I'm begging you."

My next move is to actually get down on my hands and knees on the stoop and supplicate in front of Kristy until she lets me into her bungalow.

But Kristy's too big to make me do that.

"All right, come in." She sighs like she's lending money to someone she knows'll never pay her back. "I'm so mad at you. It was so embarrassing. My mom kept shaking her head the whole time, like I'm ten years old. And not even a phone call. How long does that take? Thirty seconds to make a phone call . . ."

This is good. Honest punishment I deserve. Suddenly I'm not some sick sadochicken, I'm just some dumb schlub who messed up with his girl, like a million dumb schlubs before me. When she's railing on me I can imagine we're a couple in the middle of a spat we'll look back on years from now and laugh about.

"I know, I'm so sorry. See, I meant to tell you this. I'm . . . I was . . . *embarrassed*. And the truth is . . .

"I'm a . . .

"I've been . . .

". . . selling drugs . . ."

My mom yanks me out of Lyndon Baines Johnson Junior High when I'm fifteen, and along with about twenty other families, she decides to start a school. So we rent a house, we hire teachers, and we start the Dallas Free School.

One of the teachers is an earnest young educator out of the Midwest. Round-faced, blond, and whipsmart, she takes no guff, but at the same time she's patient and kind, a great teacher and an all-around good egg. My mother and the teacher talk more in one night than my mom and my dad talked in twenty years. She and her new best friend start attending teaching conferences, and National Organization of Women's meetings, and Gloria Steinem fund-raisers. These women are not quilting, or swapping recipes, or buying Tupperware. They're pissed off. They want equal pay for equal work, alimony payment protection, and day-care reform. They want to stop the war and feed the children. Equality, liberation, and R-E-S-P-E-C-T. They want clitoral orgasms and Freud be damned!

So my mom sings, she marches, she gets naked and feels comfortable with her own beautiful female body in deeply feminine ways no man can ever understand.

While my father is building his high-tech state-of-the-art explosives factory in Useless, Texas.

I give Kristy a tremendous song and dance about how this deal on Easter got all screwed up, and I didn't get the shit sorted out till three in the morning, and I was gonna come over then, but it was too late, and then I hadda work at the restaurant all day today, and I just got off, and as soon as I did, I came right over to apologize, and make it right.

I want to make it right. That's the truth.

Kristy knows something's off about me, she's felt it from the first day we met. She studies me. Slowly she shakes her head.

"Why would you do something like that? How can—"

I cut her off at the pass. I'm not a chicken anymore, but now I'm a drug dealer, which is not much better; plus it means I've been lying to her, which is bad. So I launch right into the whole Sunny/Dumpster/working at the restaurant/becoming a hooker ordeal (minus SEXY), only I substitute drugs for chickening.

"Why didn't you tell me?" Kristy shakes her head.

"Like I said, I was embarrassed. I'm really sorry . . . but I like you so much and I felt like such a freak . . ."

Long silence.

I wait for her to tell me to get out. Or call me over for the hug. But she just stands there and looks at me. More silence. I can hear the tumblers rolling around in her head as she tries to fit all this new information into her jigsaw puzzle of me.

"What do you want from me?" she finally says.

"I wanna have sex," somehow bolts past security and out of

my mouth. Even as it's coming out, I want to suck it back in and say something sweet, soft, and cuddly.

"You blow me off, then show up the next night, and you expect me to have sex with you? You are unbelievable."

"I'm sorry, I'm—" sinking so fast.

"I can't do it anymore. You need to go now." Kristy's made up her mind. I can see it in her spine.

"What're you saying? Are you breaking up with me?" I'm not a loverstudguy, I'm a pathetic loser who betrayed his sweet girl.

"Yes, I am. Now I'd like you to leave."

I'm done. A sneer appears from behind my ear as I disengage, pulling the switch down, the Silence descending over me.

"Whatever."

This is the last word I ever say to Kristy.

When I leave her house, something turns off inside me. I have no more Kristy. I've ejected myself in a bloody blaze of violence from the chicken industry, so I have no 3-D.

Arrest me, shoot me, I don't care anymore.

I am, of course, ravenously hungry. So I get my day-old birthday cake, my ice cream, and my milk, take it home, and shovel it all into my face with doomed fervor.

In about a week I'll get a strange sore throat from eating all that cake and ice cream for so many months, and by the time my roommate makes me go to the doctor I'll be hallucinating, burning alive at the stake of my own fever. The doctor'll tell me I have trench mouth. My mouth has become a trench. In another week to ten days, I would've been dead. The doctor'll make me get a douche bag, fill it with boiling-hot water, dissolve a pink antibiotic powder into the water, take the business end of the cord and shove the phallus as far down my throat as I can, then release the water, six times a day.

I'll never see Sunny again. He won't come looking for me, and I won't go looking for him. I'll never see any of my little freak family. But that's not unusual. People come and go so quickly in that world.

I'll see Kristy every week in Existentialism, but I'll never speak to her again.

But here, now, after I've been dumped in the Dumpster by Kristy, with yet another lactose seizure upon me, I start to see lights at the edge of my eyes, strange lights I've never seen before. At first I can't tell if the lights are really there, because whenever I look directly at them, they move somewhere else. Then a pain strikes inside my head, like someone's drilling a thin diamond bit into my brain with each breath I take, knocking me down on the bed with nausea.

Then I'm asleep.

When my father suspects his wife, my mother, is having woman's orgasms with her new best friend, he can't say, "I love you and I sense us growing apart; can you help *me* give you a woman's orgasm? Let's talk about this and work something out."

And my mother can't say, "I love you and I sense us growing apart, can you help *me* have a woman's orgasm? Let's talk about this and work something out."

So my dad wonders in denial, while my mom explores her new partner.

My mother told me once that if my father had ever once come to her while their marriage was falling apart and said, "Please, I love you, don't go," she would've stayed.

But he didn't ask.

I call my nice normal smart funny loving American friend Penny the next day. She was my girlfriend at boarding school. I ask her to come live with me when the school year's over, and to my eternal gratitude she says yes. Suddenly I don't feel compelled by a force I can't control to eat massive amounts of day-old birthday cake and ice cream.

In May, Penny comes to be with me. I don't tell her about my chickenhood, or the tall man with the SEXY shirt and what he did to my ass. I keep my secret for a decade, and when I finally do tell someone, she marries me.

Penny and I drive my bike up the coast to Oregon. We love under the stars and drink sunsets over the ocean. She's a damaged soul herself, but she gives me much love. And it turns out I'm her escape hatch, too, so while she's helping to save me, I'm inadvertently helping to save her.

We move in with my mother and her new lover. They're not happy about it, but God love them, they take me back, and continue to take me back, even after I accidentally set their couch on fire, accidentally shoot a rainbow of puke all over the side of their house from my second-story window, and accidentally do countless other dastardly deeds.

I go to college that fall. They have dorms. I live in one. Penny moves on.

When I'm thirty-five, at the suggestion of my therapist, I write each of my parents a letter describing my chicken days.

"Is this one of those wacky little stories you like to write?" asks my dad.

"No, it's not," I say.

Then we hang up.

"David, what do you really want?" asks my mom.

"I want you to know," I reply.

Long pause.

"I'm sorry that happened to you. I'm sorry." That's what my mom says.

The lock breaks, the door busts open, the bats fly out, and the hole in my bucket closes.

Almost.

Acknowledgments

I would like to acknowledge my parents for all the love and support they have given me. I thank my brother for being a constant source of love and sweetness my whole life, often in the face of enormous ugliness on my part.

James Levine, president of James Levine Communications, was not only helpful as a keen, astute, and cunning business adviser, but he also helped form the structure of the book with several brilliant suggestions early on in the process. Melissa and Mike must also be acknowledged for their contributions from the office. My editor, Cal Morgan, has been a joy to work with, with his immense knowledge, his remarkable diplomacy, and his dry wit. I thank Judith Regan for taking a chance on me. Robert Shaw is the wonderful artist who designed our proposal. I thank Marion Rosenburg for teaching me so much about writing, and Greg Mahr for putting up with me for so many years.

Michael Cira must be thanked for being a great and constant

friend who has taught me much about life. Thank you to Steph for being a good friend for many years, and to Ruth and Sam for being Ruth and Sam. Judy deserves special kudos for being so patient and understanding in the face of such rampant cussedness. I thank my sisters Kate and Liz for sticking by me when I wasn't such a great brother. Ron and Craig are to be congratulated for being the most stable members of our family. Beverly should be lauded for welcoming me with open arms over and over. Rachael has been a source of joy from before she was even born. Aunty Betty Whittle was a shining light in a sea of darkness. Larry Jones lent me five hundred bucks when I needed it. Paul Hoppe took me to Ireland, and got me started writing seriously. Alex Kinney taught me everything I know. Katie Humes was very helpful in reading and giving comments and being kind and wonderful. Susan Wooldridge was immensely helpful technically, spiritually, and emotionally. Louis Stein must be noted for his extraordinary contribution in the areas of humor, goodwill, and hooping. I learned much from Ron Emory at Darrow School. Josh the wolf Shenk, Jack Haley, and Laura Sedlock were kind enough to read for me, and gave me excellent suggestions and feedback. Marcia Hurwitz helped me in more ways than she knows. Karen Leslie and David Sharps taught me about how to be seriously foolish. Iggy Breninkmeyer, Pascal, Irene, and Kylie were kind enough to let me sleep on their couch. Susie Greenebaum let me spread like an invading virus in her apartment as I wrote this. Janine Weissman helped me to get better.

Tina Jacobson must be singled out twice. Once, for being a brilliant agent who took a lump of coal and crafted a diamond out of it. Then for being a brilliant friend who gave a crazy mad-as-a-hatter novel to her goddaughter, the agent. Thanks for everything, Tina. You are a rare and lovely human being.

Which brings us to the mother lode. The goddaughter of Tina. The one and only Snow Leopard herself, the apple in my coffee, the cream in my eye: Arielle Eckstut. Besides being the greatest agent I've ever had by leaps and bounds (and I've had more agents than any human should have), and having the insight to take said novel and suck the truth from it, she is also a gorgeous beauty, a walking Zagat's Guide, an avid animal lover, a wild animal, a deep thinker, a profound wit, the best of friends, a very good driver, a wonderful writer, an expert Austenian, an inquisitive explorer, and a sweet and loving human of the highest order. Even living to be 120, I will never be able to thank her enough.

Finally, I'd like to issue a general apology to the many people who are owed one. The following people have helped me, and I would love for them to contact me at *sterryhead@earthlink.net,* or through my publisher.

Carter Mitchel	Leon Johnson	Laura Greer
Cathy Holmes	Victoria Emory	Serena DiPinto
Jenny Robinson	Richard Buchsbomb	Alice Guerrero
Tracy Ellis	Arnolpho di Mello	
David Piscuscus	Lee Scroggins	